Anonymous

Amat

Vol. III

Anonymous

Amat
Vol. III

ISBN/EAN: 9783337040444

Printed in Europe, USA, Canada, Australia, Japan

Cover: Foto ©ninafisch / pixelio.de

More available books at **www.hansebooks.com**

AMAT.
VOL. III.

A M A T.

A Novel.

IN THREE VOLUMES.
VOL. III.

LONDON:
CHAPMAN & HALL, Limited, 11, HENRIETTA ST.,
COVENT GARDEN.
1881.

(Late 193 Piccadilly.)

Bungay:
CLAY AND TAYLOR, PRINTERS.

AMAT.

CHAPTER I.

"Well, well, he was the covert'st sheltered traitor that ever lived."—*Buckingham*.

SINCE the conference in Eaton Square, Adéle's life had run in pleasanter lines so far as Clarice could affect it, and for a time she was more nearly happy than she had been during her exile. But at length she began to see that though Archie came more regularly to the house she saw less of him alone, for on one pretext or another they very rarely had an interview which was not of the briefest. And when once she rather timidly suggested a walk, he reminded her of the necessity of meeting Miss Beauchamp's ideas of propriety with a gravity which threw an unaccustomed chill over the poor girl's impulsive heart.

In truth, Master Archie, whose feelings had never been more than momentarily touched by the passionate demonstrations of the untutored Adéle, had become more than ever the slave of the unconscious Clarice, who, accepting him cordially in the *rôle* of Platonic friendship which he had so skilfully adopted, ever welcomed him with a warmth of manner which made him, moth-like, only the more eager to make the flame his own, even though at a risk which he knew was all but mortal.

At times, utterly devoid as he was of vanity, and self-abasing as a man truly in love must be, he thought that if he could but drive Charlie from her thoughts even for a little, he might win a place from which eventually he could gain her heart. And, as his pulse beat quickly, and his brain grew dizzy with the maddening hope of making her his own at last, his better angel left him finally, and he determined at any cost to gain his end.

Is Lucifer ever on the watch to seize us at our weakest moments and aid the temptation with the opportunity? It too often seems so.

Hardly has Archie decided, *coûte que coûte*, to sacrifice his cousin and his *protégée* in order to achieve his purpose, when the inviting downward path opens before him.

Looking in at Wilton Place one morning, he finds his sister Olive alone, deep in the perusal of a letter from her *fiancé*.

Colouring, as she puts it hastily in her pocket, she embraces her brother with unusual effusion.

"Hulloa, Ottle! Why so liberal in your salutes to-day? Are you told by the gallant Fergus to keep up the exercise, in safe quarters, during his absence?"

"Hardly, sir; but he says something in his letter which I think may have a deeper interest for you."

"Really!"

"Yes; you remember Amy, and her desperate attempts on Charlie's heart? Well, it seems that she is spending her widowhood at a place called Nainee Tal. What took her there, when her husband was killed hundreds of miles from there"—Olive's geography is not practical—"and her natural plan would have been to come home, you may best understand when I tell you that Charlie has been invalided to the same place, where everyone is scandalized by the way in which this newly-made widow is throwing herself at his head."

"Phew!"

"You may well whistle. Poor Clarice evidently knows nothing of all that is going on, for she supposes he is only getting well to come home. Yet, if she has any spirit she will not stand this state of things when she hears of it. Fancy being supplanted by that red-haired chit who tried so long in vain to be her rival at home!"

"Soh! But who is to tell her, my Ottle?

She might either be majestically supercilious, or so cut up that I don't know which I would choose not to witness if I were the bearer of the news."

"Our ancestor did not hesitate to bell the cat when occasion demanded."

"True; but, you know your own sex best, don't you think that it would be a mistake for me to hint at a knowledge of her engagement? I have always studiedly ignored it."

"Of course. Surely you do not need me to tell you how to use your cards in a game you have played so often. If, as I believe, you wish to win Clarice, you never had such a chance as now. What help I can give you I will. I know Charlie has not written to her for an age, but he has mentioned Amy repeatedly to his mother. It will be strange if you cannot with such materials work up doubts in her mind which you can turn to your own advantage."

Now Olive was by no means a bad-hearted girl in the original, but the doctrine instilled by her mother so sedulously had borne its evil fruit; and, seeing how essential it was for Archie to be successful in his matrimonial venture, which his sisters had often discussed, she had no scruples in trying to bring to an end the engagement, so that not only might her brother's plans be advanced, but possibly her sister helped in the great scheme of her mother's later life.

"I confess I was so impressed with the idea of her devotion to him that I had almost given up the idea of being able to shake her faith."

"The very reason, most obtuse brother, why the shock of hearing that he is faithless should make her heart rebound, when you may catch it."

"And if I fail?"

"As a soldier you should know that if you go into action thinking so much of defeat you are little likely to be victorious."

"*Ma foi!* You should apply for a Professorship at the Staff College. Tactics are evidently your *forte*."

"Seriously, Archie, if your visions of Clarice,

Champ Royal, a seat in the House, etcetera, are ever to be realized, you had better lose no time. The season is getting on—and—"

"But I shall see her at Amat, and have her much more to myself than is possible here."

"Yes, in a sense; but don't you think that there her heart and mind will go back to last year, and that the tender passages thereof will be dreamt over to the utter destruction of your chances?"

"I recant. You should have been a barrister!"

"Nonsense. Be in earnest for a moment, or I will let you 'gang yer ain gate.' I am going to Clarice presently. I will read from Fergus's letter the Indian news, which she will be very glad to hear, and will only stop when I have got so far as to make her anxious to know more of those picnics and boatings at Nainee Tal, which I must honestly confess I should not like to think were reported of my own betrothed. For the rest, I must leave you to sow where I have harrowed. 'Twill be for you to reap."

"I see. Well, I'll try."

"Why, you speak, Archie, as if I were suggesting something distasteful. You don't mean to say," she said, turning suddenly upon him as a thought flashed across her, "that you have let your heart be touched by that dark-eyed panther you brought over from Paris? I have not been blind to her *minauderies*, but I gave you credit for more sense than to be caught by them!"

"And you are right, most sagacious sister. I can truly say that Clarice's little finger is more to me than the whole of poor Adéle."

"Why 'poor'?" she asks quickly.

"Because I am sorry for her. She is alone, poor child. In the whole world there is not a soul possibly who cares for her."

"Take care, most self-reliant brother. Pity is dangerously akin to love, for such things as pretty women; and she is one, undeniably," says Olive viciously; for she has long feared an entanglement in that quarter.

"That may be; but, since you are for the time my Mentor, what am I to do?"

"Oh, you brothers!—I wonder if husbands will be as trying?"

"Heavens! You do not contemplate polyandry?"

"You, possibly, are a good deal nearer polygamy! If you take my advice, you will let Adéle return to her own people without further delay. I confess I distrust her. Follow up any advantage you may gain by Clarice's confidence in Charlie being shaken, and make your arrangements to be as much in her society as you can in the autumn."

"I will, and I won't stand upon the order, but do it quickly. To-night I shall see her at the Queen's ball, and in the mean time I will try and find out from Gibbie Elliot if his brother has told him what fire there is to produce Fergus's smoke."

Left alone, Olive is satisfied that she has done well in laying a train to assist her brother and sister in trying to obtain what she had learned to consider the great object in life—a satisfactory matrimonial market for their own wares, irrespective of the ruin their success might inflict on others.

Meanwhile Archie proceeds to the club, where he knew he would find Elliot a temporary prisoner through being on guard.

"Heard lately from your brother, Gibbie?"

"Yes; got a letter this morning. He seems to like himself pretty well at Nainee Tal, and raves about the scenery."

"There's not much society, I fancy?"

"No. At least he never mentions anyone but two ladies, with whom they seem to be rather thick."

"Who are they?"

"Mrs. Bolton, the wife of some fellow down in the plains, and a Mrs. Gardenne, cousin of Grant's, rather a gay one to have been so lately a widow, I gather."

"Why? Is she making raids on Ronnie's inflammable heart?"

"I fancy not. She seems to set her cap at her cousin, who apparently finds it not an unpleasant relationship. I shouldn't wonder if it ends in her hooking him. A state of convalescence and idleness in such a climate, coupled with propinquity to a pretty face always on the look-out for you, are heavy odds against any man."

"So she is good-looking, this fair cousin?"

"Ronnie says he has seen nothing like her but the picture of Mary Stuart at Saxbury. If so she must be very dangerous."

"Perhaps he is himself a victim!"

"Not likely. In the first place I fancy he is pretty well gone in another quarter at home. And he is not the sort to try and cut out a pal."

With which unintentional facer, Elliot, who has no great love for Archie, puts on his bearskin and goes back to the Tilt.

"By Jove!" mutters Archie, "if it has gone so far as to be a question of cutting out, she must have fetched him after all, and I may go in for the other with a clear conscience."

Olive, with the iron hot before her, resolves to lose no time in striking.

Weeks have grown into months since Clarice wrote her penitential letter; yet the time so anxiously looked for, when his reply might have come, has passed. There has been no loving response, such as she made sure of. On the contrary, his letters to his mother seemed tinged with a bitterness quite unlike him. Then came his wounds and illness, it was true, but since then he had recovered enough to go to the Hills, and write to his mother frequently—yet not to her! What can it mean?

Not a word of all she suffers has she breathed to Lady Amat or Eila; and with a brave heart she has loyally concealed, even from her mother, every outward sign of doubt or sorrow, beyond the natural ones she showed on hearing of his danger. But at times the task is almost beyond her strength, and she seeks to distract her thoughts in the unhealthy excitement to which Archie knows well how to administer the poisonous stimulant; an anodyne daily becoming more necessary to her, involving, as it does, the almost constant society of him from whom she takes it, interwoven with whom, in an inexplicable manner, are the fibres of her tenderest thoughts for Charlie.

Thus the smoke arises on this side of the widening gulf.

Eila, wondering indeed, looks on in silent sorrow. She sees, but feels that interference cannot mend such matters — the more so when she hears from more than one of the Campbell family a confirmation of Gilbert Elliot's passing joke about Charlie's danger with the widow.

It makes her sympathetically sad; for if, she thinks, such plighted troth as theirs can so little stand the strain of time and separation, what hope has she of finding her reliance on unspoken words rewarded?

Clarice, knowing an Indian mail has come in

that morning, again without a word for her, is sitting alone with a heart full of many disturbing thoughts, when Olive is announced.

"I thought I would look in for a moment, dearest, in case by any chance you have no news." Poor Clarice shivers, imperceptibly almost, but, enough for her quick-eyed visitor to see she has touched the suspected sore. "I have such an amusing letter from Fergus, who is bearing the heat of Bareilly wonderfully, he says They seem to have made themselves very comfortable with thatched roofs on the ruined bungalows, and ladies are arriving in the place, so they have some of the amenities of life. Though I hear such terrible tales of the fascinations of the Indian dames, that I hope he will not rush rashly into danger."

"I am very glad, Olive; the accounts of the heat in tents were terrible."

"Yes; and with the 'coolth' and other attractions of the Hills almost within their grasp, their feelings must be sometimes like those of the

Lydian king. Though, perhaps, it is as well for my happiness, if not for his, that Fergus is exposed to physical heat alone."

"You are enigmatical this morning, Olive!" says poor Clarice, with a smile that barely conceals the sinking heart. She feels a blow is coming, which, dreading, she is too proud to shrink from.

"Am I? Perhaps it's better to be ambiguous than ambidexterous. I was only congratulating myself that my *fiancé* is not finding the mischief so metrically told us in our childhood as the result of idleness. For I know our sex well enough, my dear, to be doubtful of a man's strength when exposed to charms which are greater, in his eyes perhaps, than the distant ones legitimately his own."

"With such sentiments, you are fortunate indeed!" is the calm, incisive answer.

With a pertinacity which would be brutal did not her grosser nature prevent her conceiving half the torture she is inflicting. Olive, stung by the retort, says, "How glad you must be, dearest, that Charlie has such a safety-valve in Amy! With her, of course, there can be no danger; though the gossips, probably envious and ignorant of their relationship, have evidently thought otherwise."

Too proud and self-controlled to betray her emotion, Clarice listens to the end with an outward calm, which, deceiving the less self-disciplined Olive, takes away any scruples she may have felt, and believing that after all Charlie has returned to his *premier amour*, she seizes the welcome thought that Clarice, caring less for him than she had imagined, has already allowed her heart to incline towards her brother.

Pale as she has been increasingly of late, Clarice says Good-bye, with a radiant self-possession which makes Olive congratulate herself on her success, and as she drives away she thinks:

"She could not have cared so much for him after all! Archie need not have been so very doubtful of his winning her. It's the old story.

Faint heart never did succeed. The question is, Should he wait?"

But Clarice! Hardly has the door shut when she sinks back and weeps those bitter tears which are wrung from us, not so much by sorrow as by the stinging sense of helpless wrong, of undeserved hurt, from the hand we thought so incapable of dealing us aught but love.

"Is it, can it be true?" she keeps on murmuring. "Is this the cause of all his cruel silence? Have I all my life long wasted my love on one who professed to give me an equally true and enduring devotion! Oh, Charlie! surely it cannot be! If you but knew how I have loved you, you could not have caused me such pain as this." And then with characteristic unselfishness she begins to make excuses for him.

Amy, of whom his letters to his mother since he went to Nainee Tal have been full, had been his child-love ere she herself had gone to Amat. Everyone spoke of her excessive beauty now.

Why should she not awaken the tender feelings which were probably only dormant in her absence?

But in the attempt to defend him she opens her own wounds afresh; and, overcome by their uncontrollable agony, she is surprised in tears by Adéle, entering in an evidently perturbed state herself.

Affecting not to notice her emotion, she says: "*Chére mademoiselle*, I have a note from Colonel Campbell, asking me to tell you he wishes to see me on a matter affecting my future. You know how much I owe to his kind thoughtfulness. May I say he can come here?"

"Certainly, Adéle. Where else? I hope it may be to give you good news."

"*Pauvre enfant!*" thinks Adéle, as she goes back to her own room. "Have you even begun to learn that the sun may darken before noon, be the morning ever so bright? I wonder if that handsome *Montagnard* they all rave about has been playing her false? I know she has not had an Indian letter for months. Stay!"—and she buries her rounded chin in her soft hand, while many thoughts flash through her brain. "Ah! Monsieur Louis, have you all this time been playing a double game? We shall see to-morrow."

Seizing a pen, she writes rapidly to him. What is there in the words which makes him wish that "to-morrow" was over?

Punctually to the hour his soldier instincts bring him to the house where he feels a crisis awaits more than himself.

"Ah, *mon ange!*" he exclaims, as springing from his chair he attempts to embrace Adéle, who has purposely kept him waiting some few minutes.

But she, for the first time since their intimacy has grown to the stage of endearments, skilfully evading his salute, gravely motions him back to his seat, saying:

"Is it not time for an *éclaircissement?* How long is it since you told me that you loved me?

—that if I wished for happiness I must obey you in all things? Have I not done so? I confess I do not understand many things. Your professions of devotion, are they not at variance with the reality? But I forgot! You had something to say affecting my future! What is it?"—and the concluding words ring out with a *fierté* which reminds him of her long-forgotten father.

Infinitely relieved by the opening she has given him so unexpectedly, he replies, in reproachful tones: "Adéle, you forget, I think, many things! Is it not true that I pointed out long ago the difficulties in the way of our love running smooth? I am not rich, though you may well think otherwise; and I am not able to marry you at all hazards. I must wait. If the trial on your patience or affection be too severe, say so frankly, but do not seek to cast the blame upon me, my want of purpose or devotion."

In an instant every doubt for herself, every thought of others, which has made her desperate, and for the moment so repellent to him, is flung to the winds, and the impulsive girl is sobbing on his breast while he calms the self-reproachful storm of sobs which his well-chosen words have evoked.

He feels that a danger he cannot measure has just been narrowly escaped, and that a recurrence must be avoided at all hazards. He is aware that Clarice has not written to Charlie for a length of time, which, coupled with his known silence to her, shows that the breach in their correspondence is complete, and that the cats-paw may be dispensed with as no longer necessary.

"Ah, mon Louis!" cries penitent Adéle, who mistakes his cogitative silence for continued displeasure. "Can you forgive me? I am indeed an *ingrate* to doubt you. But oh! you do not, cannot know, how I live when you seem cold or distant, or needlessly long absent! What would you? You are my very all now." And, lifting up her face, she kisses him again and again, as if seeking to recompense herself for her enforced abstinence; until at last even Archie's cold, calculating nature is warmed by her beauty and passionate caresses into a response which satisfies the love-hunger of the fervidly-devoted woman.

At length he says: "Adéle! you will not again doubt me if I do or suggest that which you may not at the moment understand?"

"Try me, *mon cœur*."

"I must. I have long seen, and this day has proved, that our present position is a false one in many ways. I think there is only one way of altering it."

"And that, *chéri?*"

"Is by your returning to France, where you will be less fettered in some respects than here."

"I would rather be in a prison, *mon amour*, if you were my jailor, than free as air where you were not."

"I am only going to open the door that I may

be the more able to join you, *carissima*. At first we may be at a greater distance than that which now separates us; but I will soon be with you in Paris, and then better able to arrange our future. I can see your relatives, who may not refuse to give their consent to what will add to your happiness."

"Ah, Louis, do with me as you will. You know you have only to speak and I will obey. Give me but the hope that I shall see you and be with you always and I will bear anything."

"Then I may tell Miss Beauchamp that you wish to return to your aunts?"

"Why not? Only, Louis, if you do not wish me to die, send me not there to live without seeing your face and hearing your voice yet more often than I have of late."

"I promise."

"*Mon bien aimé!*" cries Adéle, flinging her arms round him as if she would impart her warmer nature to his less demonstrative one; "send me quickly then, for sometimes I feel as if this air of England were killing me with its cold fogs and colder forms which shrivel all my joyous life until I cannot breathe;" and the cough which has been her torment of late reminds him that her mother died a victim to the fell disease.

CHAPTER II.

"Knavery's plain face is never seen till used."—*Iago*.

ONCE more Amat sees the re-assembling of a section of London society, as there gather the Beauchamps, Trevors, Eversleighs, and Campbells, Ralph Mostyn, Montie Drummond, Victor Murray, Gibbie Elliot, and his father, who, having re-established himself with Lady Fanny, has resumed his old familiar friendship with the Clayshire circle, and, by consequence, the Amats.

For some of them it was impossible to feel the light-hearted gaiety with which the year before they had revelled in the keen enjoyment of life that fills most of us in breathing the stimulating air of sea and hill, and lifts us for a time out of those grosser feelings inseparable from continued struggles in the great human hive.

With not a little anxiety, Lord and Lady Amat had arrived some few days before their guests so that they might get over the dreaded interview with Hamish.

On both occasions when they had to write and tell him how they felt they owed the life of their beloved son to the unsurpassed devotion of his own, his answers showed the truth of the feeling with which he had bid them go with 'the Master' and die for him if needs be, when first Charlie had gladdened all their hearts by wearing the uniform of the Red Highlanders before he joined.

Except for the stoical pride of the grand old man it would have been almost impossible for Lady Amat to have undergone the necessary meetings to which she had looked forward with increasing dread.

Yet, when they went down to the yacht at Muirtown lock and got on board, his face, lined and saddened as it was, lit up with an affectionate greeting which needed no words, as he touched his cap, to reassure them both that irretrievable as was his loss he had no selfish thought of sorrow, but rather that of joy, since they were not childless, thanks to his brave boys.

"Welcome, me leddy. 'Tis happee tat Hamish is too see you pack again tis day."

" Ah, Hamish!" she says, extending eagerly to him her hand, which he touches as reverently as if it had been that of an empress. " My heart is too full to speak to you just now. I can only say that though I am yet a mother it is with a terrible sadness that I think at what a cost to you that happiness has been purchased."

As she goes below the old man's eye glistens, his heart leaps to his throat, and for a moment he is more nearly moved than any one has yet seen him, when his Chief, laying his hand affectionately on his shoulder, says, " Hamish! my friend of many happy, trying, and tried days, I am no better able than Milady was to thank you; but, as you know, since we are of the clan, we are not less than kin, I would be more than kind."

For answer Hamish, taking off his cap, seizes Lord Amat's hand, and kissing it, much to the astonishment of the gaping, passing tourists, says rapidly in Gaelic :

" The Chief surely can do as he will with his own. Whatever was, is, or may be, I cannot love him more or less. Evan and Duncan are happy since they died for the Master, and I would not have them back ; nay, rather would I that Donald and Alastair should follow than the young Chief should fail to come home to you."

" I know, Hamish," answers Lord Amat, in their native tongue, as they walk aft together. " Yet it is impossible for us to accept such sacrifices without feeling and saying that what we owe to you and yours is more than we can even thank you for."

" It was written, as I told you that night when I was, by God's mercy, able to save the Master. If it be that my old eyes shall see him home again, think you that I shall not share your joy? Is not that enough?"

Long as they had lived together, the two Highlanders, of a school not too often met with now, feel as their hands meet in most expressive grasp that they had never before fully gauged each other.

During the run home through Loch Ness, the canal, and Loch Eil, reminding them so forcibly of what might have been, the skipper becomes himself again, and when they go ashore the few heart-felt words from each are enough to show them all that a common tie binds them indissolubly.

They are greeted by the arrival of an Indian mail, bringing a letter for his mother from Charlie full of their pleasant life at Nainee Tal.

Unacknowledged even to herself, Lady Amat's feelings for Amy had never been so partial as to Clarice in their later girlish days. It might have been due to prevision, but the result was that she had not viewed with favour her evident predilection for Charlie, and she rejoiced, secretly, when, Clarice usurping the first place in his affections, Colonel Gardenne carried off one whose increasing undeniable beauty of unusual type had frequently caused the maternal heart to quake with ill-restrained fear. Mothers have their fancies in such, as other, cases.

It was then with a vague feeling of apprehension that she read of the daily life of intimacy, so frankly revealed in Charlie's letters, between the cousins, whose earliest memories must be stored with many a loving thought, and of his sympathy with her loneliness in a far distant land becoming so acute that he now suggests her going to Amat as a home to which he might bring her when he is able to obtain leave.

"Has the boy been bewitched by her after all?" Lady Amat asks herself that night of her arrival at home, as she sits alone in the tapestried room, which recalls such vivid impressions. "Men are strange creatures; even the most loyal seem to have something of the ancient patriarchs left in them, or forget temporarily, sometimes, the women they infinitely prefer when in the presence of another who chooses to flatter them by real or assumed devotion. Oh, my son, can it be that you have forgotten or under-estimate the value of the priceless gem you deemed yourself so fortunate as to win so short a time ago?"

Fatigued by her journey, her interview with Hamish, and the anxious surmises called forth by Charlie's letter, the weary mother goes to rest wondering if Clarice's arrival next day will throw any light on a state of things which she feels may blight her views of happiness for her son, as well as for one who has become most dear to herself.

The following afternoon, when Lord Amat with Hamish and his gig's crew meet the Beauchamps, who this time elect the west coast steamer from the south, Clarice remembers keenly how they had last landed in the sheltered bay where the 'Cygnet,' trim and smart as ever, rides so easily, as if she were only waiting to spread her wings and sweep over the waters, which seem to smile a rippling welcome to the accepted daughter of their liege lord.

Though the ties between Lady Amat and Clarice had been drawn yet closer when the news of Charlie's grievous wounds and danger had so terrified them, yet there had since grown up, imperceptibly and unconsciously, a feeling of reserve in speaking of him which neither would have allowed the other to think possible had she been questioned.

As the hardest stone may be worn by continual drops of water, so may the most perfect trust of lover, wife, or mother, be corroded by almost intangible inuendoes, so hard to lay hold of or rebut without in some measure, as it were, admitting the possible truth of the inferred reproach.

Thus the Campbells, with a persistent partizanship worthy of a better cause, had for long lost no opportunity of magnifying and distorting the apparently harmless gossip which Fergus had in all innocence given in his letters to Olive, touching "the beautiful cousin," whose relationship every one had envied Charlie from the day of the unexpected meeting at Cawnpore.

All know how difficult it is to fill up the expected pages of a letter by a foreign mail, and such details as the Doctor and the Weasel gave of Amy's appearance and manner at Bareilly and Nainee Tal, supplied, through Fergus's unvarnished sheets, the requisite amount of truth to make the fables, which reached Clarice in various ways, so difficult to disprove to her own mind; though none of her tormentors had reason to congratulate themselves on having wrung from her a look or an expression which they could distort into being condemnatory of either Charlie or Amy.

Following up his interview with Adéle, Archie had lost no time in removing one serious element of difficulty in the path he had determined to follow, and found at once that, willing as Clarice had always been to make things pleasant for the forlorn French girl, there was no obstacle in the way of her immediate return to her aunts, to whom after some correspondence Archie conducted the gladly consenting Adéle; for whose comfort, as well perhaps as to ease his conscience, he had made such pecuniary arrangements with the old ladies as rendered the return of their niece less trying to their resources than when it had first been mooted.

In this way he found himself at Amat, free for a time, at all events, from what of late had grown into an increasingly anxious burden, which threatened at any moment to render abortive the schemes for which he felt he had sacrificed more than he could allow himself to think of.

When, in those silent hours which come upon all but the most seared consciences, the thoughts of what would follow exposure thrust themselves before him and would not be denied, he shuddered and tried in vain to stifle the still, small voice, which had not yet left him, by specious pleadings and threadbare casuistry. But he was not fool or knave enough; and, ere he had grasped that for which he was prepared to pay the penalty, he recognized the fact that even the most perfect success would be too dearly bought.

Nemesis indeed stalked before him and would not let him shut his eyes.

When Lady Alice arrived and found Clarice looking unusually depressed she quickly surmised the cause, and the probability of the double game she had so long been playing being declared in her favour came home to her intriguing heart with redoubled force, as she remembered how nearly it seemed lost the year before, and she cast herself into what she felt might be a deciding phase with renewed vigour.

The others of the party which the Amats had selected to fill the castle had arrived in due course, and in such numbers as left the by-play to those most concerned to be carried out with comparative ease.

The Beauchamps had a suite of rooms next to

the Amats, and it was not long before Clarice found herself alone with the mother of her betrothed.

"You have heard from Charlie, darling, by this mail?" asks Lady Amat as they sit in her boudoir looking over the terrace, whence Clarice can see the very seat on which they pledged their vows of eternal truth.

"No; have you, dear?" is the answer, accompanied by a shortened breath, which, faint as it is, conveys only too great a significance to the straining ear.

"Yes; but I would give more than I can say to have him safe at home with us again."

"You fear nothing for him just now, do you?" asks Clarice, turning paler than ever as she fancies she detects a latent meaning in the tone of the wish, only too true an echo of what has been filling her heart for many an anxious day.

"No," hastily and inconsistently replies the poor mother; "but ever since I recognized the folly of my reliance on that vision which promissed so much, but which in the spirit has already been broken, I have lost that confidence which enabled me to bid him farewell with such calmness."

"Ah! you must not drift back into that state of mind, *madre mia*. It is like being at sea without a rudder. Let us not forget what great dangers he has already passed through, that he tells you that the troubles out there are nearly at an end, and that as soon as he can get leave he will come home."

"Yes. I try to comfort myself with thinking that he is, for the time at all events, exposed to no great dangers—at least physical ones. Has he mentioned his cousin Amy much to you?"

"He spoke of her in one of his letters," faintly replies Clarice, who feels that she may presently have to lay bare all that she has so long successfully hidden.

"I am vexing myself unnecessarily perhaps, childie, but I cannot help contrasting what is with what might have been; and yet—"

"Dearest 'Mum'!—what is it that disturbs you?" cries Clarice, winding her arms round her. "What is it? Tell me if there is anything that Charlie has said which makes you think he is worse than he cares to tell me."

"It is not that, my girl. I am very foolish to give way so. I have no real cause, perhaps, for any fears. Rather should I be grateful. There was a time when Charlie and Amy were continual playmates, but after a while I had little doubt who was to be my daughter, if she would consent!" replies Lady Amat, stroking her head with a loving smile.

"But you are uneasy, or you would not vex yourself. Tell me, for pity's sake, if you have reason for it. You know that then it must at least affect me no less," pleads poor Clarice, now seriously alarmed—for Lady Amat's words accord only too truly with her own dimly-formed misgivings, which, in spite of herself, arise at times.

"I cannot bear to think anything, still less

to hint at it; and I feel I have been very weak in saying so much, which implies a possibility of disloyalty to my boy. But ever since I heard that Amy was at Nainee Tal I have fretted over it, and exaggerating, by brooding over what are probably trifles, I have worked myself into a morbid state of mind which starts at every shadow, and induces me, perhaps, to give him less credit than he deserves for right feeling or self-control. But her name is in every letter, everything he does; and now he suggests her coming here for a home, as since her aunt's death she is, in her childless widowhood, without one!"

Smothering the sob that would rise, Clarice bravely struggles against her own swelling fears, and fights his battles for him—true-hearted and loving woman even in her pain.

"There may be good reasons for her going to Nainee Tal. Remember, India is not like England, either in its climate, or, at present, in the means of going or staying where you will. And if I feared the loss of Charlie's love, the very fact of his frankly mentioning her so often would reassure me. What more natural than he should see her every day in such a small place as they are living in, where, probably, there are few others they know or care for? His suggestion that you should give her a home is like his kind-hearted thoughtfulness. What more natural, if you like it? She has no nearer relations living. She was here a great deal of her younger life. For myself, I can well understand the probability of his finding her fairer to look at than me. I hear she is more than lovely. But," she adds, with a look of proud firmness which carries much comfort to her listener, "when he tells me she is preferred, I will believe it—not before."

"My brave, true-hearted girl!" is the impulsive answer. "I hope and believe he is worthy of you. It is not for me with my burden of carking experience to try and destroy the brightness of your faith. Doubtless you will have your reward. Come! let us look forward and think of the time when all this anxiety will seem to us like a dream—horrid while it lasted, and for a little after in its effects, perhaps, but still—only a dream."

Comforting as the conclusion might be to the more impressionable mother, Clarice's heart fairly sinks within her when she finds herself alone in the room full of such sweet memories, where she has dreamed such hopes of happiness, now so threatened by the overclouding fears which have found such new and startling expression.

Now she can no longer question the fact of his prolonged silence or its cause. And, as she recognizes the agonizing future his want of truth will create, her strong heart melts, and the proud head is bent in the very bitterness of sorrow under the last heavy blow which has fallen so unexpectedly upon her through his mother.

But in such as she faith and hope are not easily extinguished, though the mocking waves of envy, malice, and uncharitableness may leap up and try to quench them,—and she bears herself bravely before the others. Yet for all her courage and strength of purpose, Clarice cannot dismiss a very shrewd idea of her depression and its cause from the keen-eyed Lady Alice, who shapes her tactics accordingly.

To her credit be it said, she did not know to what depths her son had stooped. How far she might have withdrawn her countenance it would be difficult to say, but undoubtedly for her the apophthegm touching success was a truth.

Seeing that she had distilled and administered a poison, she not unnaturally attributed the state of the victim to her own handiwork; and after a family conclave in her own room her opinion was summed up in the following words:

"Make yourself as amusing and useful as you can, Archie. Avoid every possible allusion to Charlie and his cousin. Let them run before the wind as they will, they are bound to overshoot the mark as they are now sailing. You stand by to gybe at the right moment, and you will win when they are hopelessly out of the race.

"No one ought to know better than you how to deal with a woman's heart, as our fair friend's is now. When your success is sealed, it will be Julia's turn to measure strength with that girl Amy, whom I remember but a little attractive Highland filly.

"The more Charlie may have cared for Clarice the less will Amy's hold be upon him if he thinks he has lost her through it, which in decency she cannot bring to a definite issue until her widowhood has endured some time yet.

"Meanwhile those who are determined to conquer, and know how to set about it, are half-way to victory. *Allons!*"

CHAPTER III.

"But goes this with thy heart?"—King Lear.

"You are silent, Amy," says Charlie, as he stands beside her in the verandah, alone. "You are not sad?" he asks, in a tone of tenderness which has a *timbre* of passion in it she cannot mistake.

"Yes, indeed I am," she answers softly, turning her pale face towards him, and betraying in the quivering lip and swimming eye the sorrow she cannot control. "How can I feel otherwise when I think of the past, and the future? The present is too sweet to last."

The magnetic influence of those pleading eyes draws him nearer ere he says, "That which is gone can never be recalled. But it has its teaching; let us profit by it, and make what is to come our own, in common."

"Charlie!" she exclaims, startled no less by the sudden coming of what she will not misinterpret, than by the tone in which it reaches her.

"Listen, Amy, if you will," he says softly, taking the hand she has extended in her agitation as if repelling what she only fears to find an oft-repeated dream. "I fear we have both deluded ourselves"—oh, the unutterable agony produced by the quick revulsion on her suddenly uplifted heart—"and have suffered the punishment which, rightly or wrongly, falls on those who cannot see their errors until too late. Could we have been wiser a few years ago, young as we were, we might not have had the bitter experience of to-day. We fancied we were plucking fruit of the rarest sweetness! Did we not gather ashes? What have we now in our grasp—pearls?"

Poor Amy! The hope so suddenly quenched

by his opening sentence now revives, word by word as they fall from his lips, while he looks into her upturned wondering eyes, until at last she feels she cannot be mistaken now. But still she is silent. She is conscious there is more to follow.

"I know that in gazing overmuch at the dazzling sun I was blinded, and saw nothing but its brightness. Happily for me I turned my back upon the glare, and found that it is equally glad to warm the nearest basker who may choose to worship.

"Darling! need I say more? What I have to offer is yours—will you take it? Shall we look back and feel that we have climbed to the summit, where we have found true happiness at last?"

Has he a doubt about his own?

He cannot mistake the language, which coming straight from the passionate heart, as it now throbs against his, wells up and overflows the rapturously loving eyes, which tell him with electric truth the speechless bliss he has given to one who, long waiting for it, drains it with all the thirst of long-deferred fruition.

The wave of passionate fire, carrying all before it, sweeps away memories, regrets, humiliations—everything but the present supreme moment—with irresistible power, and surging up from heart to heart, and eye to eye, brings down his lips to hers in an embrace that owes mayhap some of its scorching force to the restraint which has only nursed the flame.

Leaving Charlie to follow when it seems good to him, Ronald and the Weasel make their way home to answer their letters for the English mail, going in the morning, and Paul straightway writes the following:

"*Nainee Tal, 12th August.*

"WHEN I left Amat a year ago, you said, 'If my best wishes and sincere sympathy for all you may desire can avail, they are most fully yours.'

"To-day only have I heard that the dream of

my life, until I met you, has been realized, and now I am free, as I was not then, to ask if those kindly words, which sank into my heart with the weight of their golden meaning, will now be read by you as I have dared to interpret them.

"Eila! I said then that I hoped to find you had not forgotten me if I was spared to see you again. I fancied that your eyes responded, 'If you return and seek for my love you may be able to find it.' Was I too vain?

"I cannot wait to plead as I would, at your feet, looking into your face and combatting the many objections you may well offer to one so unworthy as I am to win a pearl of such peerless price.

"But you will be merciful in your strength? You will not decide hastily against me? You will think how much I have dared to love you, and that you have dwelt in my innermost heart since we parted, at a time when I could only hope that the mists of evil complications might ere long roll away and leave the way clear for me to come openly and ask you to be my wife?

"Forgive me if I say that, whatever your decision is, I shall always be,

"Yours devotedly,

"Ronald Elliot."

It was not an easy letter to write on the spur of the moment; but, ill satisfied as he is with it, he cannot wait for happier or more elaborate expressions. It will at least tell her that he has been silent only because he could not speak, and that the reason has lain beyond his power of control.

That thought makes him remember that a letter is equally due to the one who has given him the possibility of such happiness as he hopes to win.

And again he writes:

"My dear Father,

"I hasten to thank you for the letter which has just reached me.

"You will understand with what feelings I have read the happy convictions which have penetrated your mind and removed a weight from mine, long refusing to believe that this day would not come.

"Pray do not talk of amends to me. I am well content to be accepted as your son. But, if in occupying the position given me by seniority of birth, I do not deprive Gilbert of what he might justly expect after so many years, I cannot refuse to benefit by your power to help me in attaining what has become very dear.

"You know of course the Trevors of Saxbury. I saw the daughter a good deal after we came home from the Crimea, and we were having a pleasant time of it at Amat when we were sent out here.

"I was surprised by the suddenness of the order into what was tantamount to a confession of my passion; but I only asked her for a hope that if I lived to find myself at home again less tongue-tied by circumstances, I should find she had not forgotten me.

"She was so kind as to permit me to understand, more by her manner than her words, that she took an interest in me; and I have just now written to ask her if she will be my wife.

"Frankly accepting your letter, which enables me to do this, in the spirit I believe to have dictated it, I confide my hopes of happiness to you as an earnest of my trust that henceforth we shall be not only father and son, but friends in the best sense. Will you aid me by making her acquaintance? I am very sure you will be proud to have such a daughter.

"The bracing air up here has made me pretty well all right, and when our leave is up the Plains will be very pleasant.

"Charlie Grant and I have agreed to go home ere long, when the troubles in these parts will have ended, and our own, such as they are, may have been converted into the pleasures we hope for.

"I am, your loving son,

"RONALD."

The night is well on when Charlie, his brain yet dizzy with the tornado of succeeding passions, comes to Elliot's room, soon after his correspondence is finished.

The usual forms of the Nicotian worship are duly followed with but few words, for the thoughts of both are very busy, and neither is inclined to obtrude them on his friend; yet feeling that before they part that night something must be said of what has so abruptly influenced the current of both their future lives.

At last Ronald speaks: "Forgive me, old fellow, for the pain I fear my blunder must have caused you this evening. I meant you to read my father's letter, not Gibbie's."

"It was a kind blow, though a facer at first, Paul. It effectually made the scales fall from my eyelids, and I saw not only what I have lost, but what I might gain."

"And you have not failed?" says Ronald, with a very shrewd idea of how he has spent the intervening time.

"No," is the answer; yet it has not quite the ring of the joyous wooer, coming straight from his lady's favour. "But we have agreed, under the circumstances, to wait a year. Amy is to stay with the Boltons until we leave for England, when I hope she will go to my mother; and after that—we—will—be—married. I must write to my father, and to—to—to—Miss—Beauchamp. Though she has not written to inform me of her change of mind! So good-night, Paul! I wish you once more a thousand times good luck. No fellow deserves it better."

Ronald is too occupied with uneasy doubts, as he remarks Charlie's distant manner and disjointed way of speaking, to give him more than silent thanks for his congra'ulations as he wrings his hand. He returns him none; and Charlie goes to his room.

The minutes go swiftly by, and the hours follow each other. But the head of the man, who for so many years has known neither pain nor sorrow, until of late, remains buried in his hands, where, as he entered, he has cast himself.

Who may follow the thoughts which course round and round with maddening dance in the fever-tost brain?

When the usually calm and self-possessed throw the reins on Passion's neck, she is apt to transport them into space; whence the almost certain fall is more truly awful than to the habitually airy-minded—who, light and selfish all their lives, do not lose their heads but with the ease of practice, usually maintain their seats unhurt until she returns to mundane matter.

Not so Charlie. Carried away by his bitter sense of wrong, suddenly confirmed by Elliot's letter, he took refuge in the passion which cried aloud to him, 'Come, and I will give you more than you have lost.' And now, ere her kisses are yet cold on his lips, why is it that he shrinks from the necessity of himself cutting the remaining strands of the overstrained cable which he thought so short a time before would have held in safety his love-ship, though all the winds of rivalry had conspired to wreck her?

Who can fathom the heart of man, at all times fearful and wonderful, but rarely more so than in the mingled throes of passionate love, jealousy, hatred, and remorse?

But the day dawns, and with the rising sun comes the necessity of immediate action with its penetrating clamour; and the strife-worn Charlie, rising, masterfully casts aside the clinging thoughts which through the long watches of the night have struggled hard to bid him wait; and, writing rapidly, he seals unconscious league with base schemers to bemire his name and destroy his love.

CHAPTER IV.

"How oft when men are at the point of death have they been merry."—*Romeo.*

"*Les jours se suivent mais ils ne se ressemblent pas,*" as Amy and Charlie pleasantly find in the swiftly-fleeing days which follow the declaration of their passion for each other.

Following the homœopathic motto, he cures his troubles with infinite happiness to his lovely physician, and with ostrich-like faith he blinds himself to all but what his eyes have now learned to turn to with fervent love.

But the sweetest moons must run their course, and ere a second has grown old, rumours of warlike work come up from the regiment, necessitating the buckling on of harness, and for a time at least, adieux to tender dalliance.

It was determined therefore, at the Weasel's instigation, to give a bachelor banquet, as he called it, to the ladies, Bolton being admitted for conventional reasons.

Accordingly, for days before he was hardly visible, while his khansamah had a rough time of i scouring the country in all directions to obtain such unaccustomed delicacies as might be found, and in the result it was admitted by Nita that if her husband's merits were duly rewarded, and he ever found himself Commander-in-chief, the Weasel should have at least the offer of major domoship.

It was late and very dark when this the last of their many happy gatherings came to an end; and, after putting the ladies into their jampans, Bolton cantered off on his pony to bring down a lantern.

Much to their astonishment they reached home without meeting him or the expected light, and on enquiry they found he had not been seen since they went out to dinner.

Jampanis and syces are sent out in every direction, but they do not go far, and, their yelling cries only distract each other and poor Nita, who sits waiting at the door all night for the husband who never comes.

"Ah, Terry! where can you be?" she moans for the hundredth time. A question which she and Amy, who keeps painful watch with her, dare not to answer, though at times a terrible foreboding of the truth rushes upon them and will not be denied.

At length the day breaks, and, escorted by the three Highlanders who had come up on hearing what had happened, Nita accompanied by Amy sallies forth, not knowing what horror may not be forced upon her ere they can return.

Fearing what may be in store for her, Charlie attempts to dissuade her from going with them. "You must be tired and nearly dead from want of sleep alone," he urges.

"A woman is never tired if she does not wish to be," is her answer, in such a tone as shows her resolution is irrevocable.

Step by step as they follow the path they look on either side for traces which may give a clue to the strange disappearance, which to Nita's love-directed fears bears but one terrible explanation.

At last they come to a corner where the steep descent turns at such an acute angle that even by day it is always passed with caution, for there is no protection against a fall over the khud.

Instinctively every eye looks to the edge, and there at once are seen the last marks of a horse's hoofs. There can be no doubt Bolton has gone over there.

Pale and sick with fear, Nita preserves her calmness and presence of mind.

"A rope! A volunteer!" she says, looking round with the fixed stony eyes of one sore stricken with sudden and inexpressible sorrow.

"Here are both," says the Weasel, producing several coils of stout cord, with which he had the forethought to provide himself. "Before brushing by machinery was invented small boys were useful for cleaning chimneys. My present trade may be cleaner, but I will go down first and see what is the best way of bringing him up.

"Master, you tie that end to the tree there with one of your sailor's yarns, and pay off the cord slowly as I go down. I have got a flask of brandy in my pocket." In a lower tone he adds, " Forgive my ghastly jokes; but her face made me try to divert her thoughts. I have also a whistle. If you hear one note I have found him ; if two, he is alive ; if three, which God forbid, poor *Rouge ou Noir* has played his last game."

Unable to thank him with more than looks, Nita watches the Weasel carefully preparing the rope for contingencies. Quickly fastening it round his waist, with a loop for his left arm, and a spare six feet length with a running noose, he seizes an alpenstock from one of the men, and slides rapidly down the almost precipitous khud.

In breathless silence Nita and the rest wait,

as the rope runs out, until presently there is a check.

"More line," is holloaed up the khud, followed by a shrill blast of the whistle.

"What is that?" cries Nita eagerly.

"Your husband is there," answers Charlie gravely; but before he can further shape his dreading thoughts there comes another, yet more piercing, after which there endures a silent suspense, of which happily the full meaning is unknown to the one most interested.

At length, "Haul up," shouts the Weasel.

"He lives, Mrs. Bolton," says Charlie, as with half-a-dozen other stout and anxious hands he pulls the Weasel up to the edge, but—alone!

"I have come up only for an instant, Mrs. Bolton, to relieve your mind. Your husband is alive; I might say well. He has had a marvellous escape; but for a bushy tree, on the edge of a precipice below, he must have gone with his pony, which crashed through it with its greater weight before him, to the bottom. He seems to have been more or less insensible nearly all night. I have given him some brandy, and now I am going down with another rope to make sure our joint weight will be brought up safely. I will support him with the alpenstock, for he is a little bit knocked out of time."

It was as much as the eight jampanis could do, with Charlie and Ronald's aid, to get the united four-and-twenty stone up that terrible slope.

When at length they reach the top, and Bolton is safely lying where they stand, poor Nita's strength gives way, and she would have fallen beside her husband but for Amy's timely arm.

However, a little brandy applied to both gradually brings them round, and as they rest against the inner side it is ascertained that beyond being fearfully bruised, scraped, and shaken, he is not seriously the worse for his extraordinary leap in the dark.

Presently he gives an account of it.

"Coming out of the light of your rooms I felt

so incapable of seeing any thing that I trusted entirely to the pony, which ought to have known the road pretty well. I remember coming to this corner, as it must have been, and his stopping short; but, being anxious to get on and bring the lantern quickly back, I put my heels sharply to his side, and the next instant, with a bound, I found we were both in the air! Instinctively I put out my arms, and, as eventually we thundered into the tree where Fletcher found me, we parted company, I fear, for ever. Nothing could go over that precipice and live. Poor 'Podge.' At least he died in harness, and we can wish nothing better."

With a very wistful look Nita strokes his bruised and bleeding face, while she gives the other hand to the Weasel, as she says, "I can never forget your ready and thoughtful help. You made Terence's acquaintance at the edge of one khud and have now cemented it by an act of the truest friendship at the bottom of another. How can I thank you enough?"

The Weasel is not easily disconcerted; but as he pulls his fair moustache he thinks he would rather swing over half-a-dozen precipices than see her eyes so full of pain as they have lately been.

"You overrate the little I was able to do, Mrs. Bolton. In addition to enabling me to go across country on an animal which has not touched three figures, my light weight gives me the pull of being able to test a rope with but small risk. On our Forfarshire coast it is a trick we learn in our teens to dangle between wind and water against the face of the cliffs in search of eggs and fledglings. If ever you give us the pleasure of seeing you at Craigottar I will organize an expedition, and then you will see how ridiculously easy it must be to go up and down these khuds, with a stout enough rope."

"Ah! you are, like all true heroes, unwilling to accept the fame you deserve. Perhaps you think with the nursery rhyme, 'Praise to the face is open disgrace!' but—" and she looks earnestly into his clear blue eyes, and honest, blushing, boyish face,—" I pray you may never let your brave thoughtlessness for yourself risk overmuch what I shall always think very dear."

"No fear, madam!" he answers, with a low bow to conceal the confusion created by her heartfelt words. "You have utterly spoilt me. I shall value myself so much that nothing shall now tempt me to run the risk of even a chip to china you put so high above the ordinary delf of common life!"

CHAPTER V.

"The tiger now hath seized the gentle."—*Queen Elizabeth*.

As they walk back to their quarters from mess at Bareilly, the night before the convalescents' return from Nainee Tal to join the flying column about to march into the Terai, Fergus says, "They all had a narrow shave. I doubt if any of them would have got over it but for the trip to the Hills, which, as Mackay said, was their only chance."

"Yes," answers Ian, blowing a huge cloud from his cheroot, " but I am not altogether sure that our friend Charlie comes back what he was. That lovely cousin of his has a good deal to answer for, if half what we hear be true. She seems thoroughly to have taken possession of him, from what they say. Those *blondes cendrées* are dangerous, by Jove! as they have been from the days of Herod. It matters little, be it head or heart, if they wish it! I would have backed the glorious Beauchamp for a monkey to a pony a year ago, and now—phew! presto! Master Charlie is bowled over as thoroughly as if he had never known her!"

"It is as well, perhaps, from what I hear. She has not denied herself the pleasant tributes to which her sovereignty of beauty perhaps entitled her," says Fergus, who has lately heard more than enough from the Olive-branch of the Campbells to convince him that there at least Charlie's chance of happiness is looked upon as lost.

"Ever the same!" mutters Ian, as he pitches his weed away viciously. "I am hanged if I believe that cant about absence; except as the French put it. You're all right, old fellow," he adds presently. "You have drawn a prize, I believe, in the grand lottery, as it is well called;

but I fancy she looks upon you as more, or less, than mortal. Take care to keep up the delusion as long as you can. It don't last much, I fear, after matrimony has clipped the wings of fancy."

"You old humbug! What do you know about it? You need not be so bitter, and it's not so very long since I thought you not quite indifferent to bright eyes and discriminating smiles."

"Psha!" says Ian, somewhat hotly. "They are well enough if you can hug yourself with the belief that they are all your own."

"Ho! comes the wind from that airt, *mon ami!* But what made you think they were not?"

"I don't know why I should make you my confessor," retorts Ian; "but perhaps I had better," he adds in a quieter tone, as a grave look passes over his face and startles Fergus by its ominous intensity. "I should not like it to be thought that I was as variable as she. I admit that I was hard hit by Julia until one or two things cropped up at Amat from her mother and from herself, showing that the Master was their real game, and that it was only as a *pis aller* she allowed herself to be amused by me."

"That's a serious thing to say," says Fergus, thoughtfully. "Of course I know Lady Alice is a thorough woman of the world, and would always go in for the biggest matrimonial fish she could hook, but I think you do Julia hardly justice."

"Perhaps, old fellow. I should not like to say anything hard about Olive's sister to you. Only if it be ever said, and I am not to the fore to contradict it, that I played fast and loose with her, you will know the truth, and can tell it if you will, for my sake."

"May there be no such need, Ian, from any cause, even selfishly speaking; for, as it is, I have a difficult task before me in what I am asked to say to Charlie when opportunity offers."

"I guess it; and I do not envy you, or him, poor chap! Give him a little breathing-time after his descent from lunacy bliss. Unless I am much mistaken he will feel it horribly. One cannot change those things altogether like old clothes!"

"Happily for us all, perhaps. But in his case, as we know, it might be said with the song, 'There ne'er can be a new love, for the old love is the new.'"

"You're as full of sentiment as ever, Fergus! But stick to it! It will never play you such tricks as passion."

"*Cela dépend!*" thinks Fergus, as they turn in.

It was a glorious morning when the Highlanders, Punjaubees, and Horse Artillery pitched their camp on one of the picturesque maidans near the Sarda, the fords of which their flying column was told off to watch, and thus bar the egress of the Nana and his followers, who were known to be lurking in the dense forests at the foot of the Nepaulese Himalayas.

As they march through the jungly country the sporting instincts of all were sharpened by the strange sounds and sights which saluted them through the night and in the early morning.

A favourite hunting-ground, and much sought after by those who love the chase mingled with danger, the Terai has long been famous for glorious uncertainty as to the nature of the game which might be found at any moment. And now, owing to the mutiny, everything had enjoyed a jubilee, and accordingly increased in number and boldness.

Thus the jungle-fowl swarmed and crowed in all the beautiful audacity of their plumage and bantam-like character; while snipe, ducks, geese, peafowl, hares, black buck, cheetul, and sambur, showed themselves or their traces on every side, and at night the camp shook with the answering roar of the surrounding tigers.

" This must be the very place old Trevor made us dream of, Paul," says Ian, as several of them lounge in the pleasant shade of a spreading pepul tree.

"It looks 'shikar' all over. But here's the man who can tell us all about it," answers Ronald, as the magistrate of the district canters up on his corky little Arab.

One of the old school, with his lactean food he had imbibed an interest in the country he was destined to rise in. Filled at Haileybury with the traditions of the governing class from which he sprung, he had all the instincts of the gentleman with his tact and kindliness, so far outweighing, with the perceptive Native, the doubtful merits of the pedantic product of crude and hasty legislation—"the competition wallah."

"Well come, Fyall. We are all devoured with a thirst for blood—of tigers. You can put us in the way, we know," says Charlie, as they cluster round the flea-bitten grey.

"I have come in partly with that very object. I have secured the best local shikaris, howdahs from some zemindars about, and a few good steady elephants. For the rest, you can get the commissariat ones as beaters, if you'll stand the consequences of an accident to them."

"Agreed!" is the unanimous shout.

"Well, I'll do all I can for you, gladly; but I cannot promise grand sport, for it's much too early for the legitimate business. While the grass is thick, long, and green, and he can find plenty of water, the tiger has no fixed abode. It's only when the great heats have withered the undergrowth and dried up the pools until they become few and far between, that well-known localities can be pointed out as certain finds."

"We'll risk all that," says Ian. "If we stay here a few days everything will have travelled miles away. Can we go to-morrow?"

"Certainly. Let us make an early start, for as it is we must go some distance, and the sagacious hatti is not an animal who will hurry himself, in a general way."

Accordingly, next morning there assembles a party of seven, including Charlie, Ian, Fergus, and the Weasel, who, not having a battery of his own, is allowed at his urgent request to act as loader to Cameron, behind whom he sits in the howdah instead of the usual shikari.

Fyall, as good on a horse and in the shires as in command of a tiger expedition, for which his experience and knowledge of the language admirably adapt him, takes post in the centre as leader; Ian and Charlie appropriately put themselves on the right and left flanks, while the other four guns divide the distances of a line of thirty elephants, who form the beaters.

The thickness of the jungle and its grasses, the treacherous softness of many places *en route* to the ground, make the getting there a work of time rather trying to the impatient ones, mounted for the first time on the slow and ungainly animal whose motion is very like that of a sailing ship in a ground swell. At last Fyall holds up his *topee* as the agreed signal for silence.

Presently lifting up his rifle, the others, obeying the code, assemble round him to hear the plan he has formed.

"The herdsmen who have been out here since daybreak report that one of their cows was killed last night, not far from this. She has been only partially eaten, so there is no doubt the tiger is in the neighbourhood.

"With the jungle so thick as it is we can only beat it on chance. The great thing is to keep perfect silence. Look or listen to me. Fire at nothing, however tempting, but a tiger, and see that the mahouts keep a good line. Each gun will be responsible for the distance and dressing kept by the elephants on his right. The guns on the flanks will answer for the direction.

"One blast from my whistle will signify 'straight ahead;' two will mean 'wheel to the right,' and three 'to the left;' four prolonged ones mean 'halt.'"

Including Fyall, who had distinguished himself in the Volunteer Cavalry during the mutiny, every one of the party had seen powder burnt in anger to some considerable extent; yet as the line advances, with little noise but for the crashing of the ponderous elephantine masses through the forest, the bushes, and high waving grass which reaches nearly to the knees of the mahouts, the nerves of all are braced to the highest tension as, rifle in hand, they stand erect and eager, looking for the slightest indication of their royal quarry.

As every creature in a state of nature dreads and generally flies from the voice of man, his appointed master, and no other natural sound has the same disturbing effect, it was with some confidence that Fyall pushed on, beating in every direction for the tiger he knew would not be far away from so recent a kill.

At last they come to an oval piece of jungle, some thirty acres in extent, close to a branch of the Sarda, which runs down one side of it.

Here Fyall changes his plan of attack.

Sending the three most experienced of the shikaris in charge of the pad-elephants, he tells them to beat carefully from the further end towards the guns, whom he posts at the other, on some rising ground which interposes between the jungle and the water. If the tiger be there, he is bound to show.

They have not long to wait in doubt. Suddenly there rings out that shrill, ear-piercing, trumpet-like note which the elephant gives vent to when he winds the brute in whom he recognizes one not less potent than himself for death and destruction.

Yet minute after minute passes painfully as the excitement of expectation intensifies and nothing comes towards the guns, while the beaters approach slowly and carefully, traversing the ground from right to left like well-trained setters.

"He must be there," whispers the Weasel, as he leans eagerly forward to Fergus, standing with his rifle cocked and ready.

"Surely, unless that brute ran riot like a young hound. Stay! there is something," he answers a little too loudly, as he sees the grass move about a hundred yards in front of him.

"Soor, Sahib!" mutters the mahout, looking up reproachfully.

"Oh, only a pig after all that!" exclaims the disappointed Weasel, relapsing into a state of indifference.

But the next instant all is changed.

With a bound, which seems to take him through the air as if he were shot from a catapult, the tiger springs from the edge of the high jungle grass straight at the spot where Fergus stands posted.

Those on either side, with sportsmanlike fairness, wait for his fire and the result.

It was not long in coming, though the catastrophe was not that expected. Fergus, as cool as if he were giving the finishing stroke to a long stalk at home, takes deliberate aim, and covering the brute's magnificent chest, fires the right barrel of his heavy Purdey; but the unaccustomed pace of the charge misleads him, for the ball, striking the tiger's forehead at an angle, glances off and only makes him roar with pain and fury as he dashes yet more fiercely at the elephant. Now follows what sometimes happens from the antagonism bred by the memory of former struggles.

The elephant, lent by a Rajah himself much given to the noble sport, on hearing the roar and seeing the tiger close upon him, refuses to wait impassively, but, to the infinite horror of the others who at once see the danger, charges impetuously to meet him, trumpeting loudly, as with his trunk and tail high in the air they close with a terrible crash.

It is done so suddenly that Fergus's second barrel goes into empty space as the howdah rocks and reels, while their mount, maddened with the rage born of fear, dashes forward.

The mahout sticks manfully to his seat, shouting continuously, while he belabours the infuriated beast with his iron mace—but with no apparent effect; and ere the other guns can fire with safety, the elephant and tiger meet in mutual charge!

At the instant of impact the latter bounds

fiercely off the ground, to which he seemed about to be pinned by the gleaming tusks, and alights on the head and trunk of his adversary.

Leaning forward, Fergus, with a promptitude and nerve which delight Fyall, who has seen not a few such combats in his time, is just going to deliver his fire down the tiger's throat as it yawns its hideous depths before him, when the elephant throwing itself suddenly on its knees, in its endeavours to shake off or crush the torture-producing burden, pitched the occupants of the howdah over its head.

For a few moments there is a struggling mass towards which the friends of the unfortunate men dare hardly turn their eyes, as they see the frantic efforts of the huge brute to rid itself of the clinging beast which, cat-like, seems to fix its claws yet deeper in the sensitive flesh, while Fergus and the Weasel lie motionless beneath them.

Fyall, seeing that in his agony the elephant must trample on the prostrate men if the struggle continues, chooses the lesser danger, fires, and, happily smiting the tiger fairly on the shoulder, forces him to let go his grasp.

Gradually relaxing all his hold, the mighty brute sinks back, and falls close by to Fergus, just beginning to recover from his stunning fall. Seeing the coming danger, he stretches out his arm instinctively to ward it off, and the fierce beast, seizing it in his jaws, draws him into his fell clutches.

It was at this supreme moment, when all hope of saving their friend seems impossible to the others, that the Weasel's senses happily return; and as he staggers to his feet the first thing he sees is the tiger on his side close to him, with poor Fergus in his grasp, his left arm crushed and mumbled by the half-unconscious monster.

While in the Hills the Weasel had seen the Ghoorkas strike off the head of a bullock by one sweep of a hukari, and made himself soon after the possessor of one of those formidable knives, which he had belted round his waist that morning.

Drawing it without a thought of self, he dashes in at once, and using all his strength, he strikes the tiger full on the neck behind the ear. Instantly the jaws relax, and Fergus is released; but, alas! in the convulsive effort of expiring nature the muscular limbs contract, strike out with mighty force, and the Weasel is hurled back a victim to their cruel power and his own selfless pluck.

By this time the other guns had got their elephants close to the fatal scene, and, descending quickly from their howdahs, hurried to the rescue.

What has taken some few minutes to relate, was enacted in a briefer space of time, and none of the efforts which were made could have prevented the terrible mishap, though while the two poor fellows lay lifeless on the ground, the others as they came up reproached themselves bitterly for not having performed the impossible.

"Poor Fergus!" says Ian, as he kneels beside him, bathing his clammy forehead, while a little brandy is forced between his clenched teeth. "It is hard lines on you to go down like that! Is there any hope for him, Fyall? His arm is very much of a jelly, but I see no other wounds."

"His pulse begins to beat," cries Charlie; "and if we could get him quickly back to camp before his senses return he will be saved the pain of the jolting."

"Bind his arm up as high as possible to stop the bleeding, if you can," says Fyall; "while I'll find out the elephant with the easiest motion. He had better be strapped on a pad, it does not jerk so much as the howdah, and one of you can sit beside him to hold up his head. The fastest of the lot had better be off to camp and let them know. His arm must go. I trust it may be no worse, but those tiger wounds are bad things to get over. How's the boy?"

"I fear he's done for," answers Charlie, as they lay him down, after having tried in vain to find any token of life. "It must be all internal, for there's not a scratch upon him."

The Doctor's kindly face lengthens as after a careful examination he holds a consultation with his subs.

"There's no hope for Cameron," he whispers, "unless we sacrifice his arm at once. 'Tis the only thing to avoid mortification, if not tetanus."

"*Bis dat qui cito dat*," says one of them, anxious to show his Aberdonian Latin to his chief.

"I wud tak anither verrb, gin I were tae crack that langwidge, whan a puir fallie's bonnie airm was taen aff," disapprovingly remarks the not unlettered hospital sergeant, as he grimly carries away what was Fergus' bridle-hand.

From the first, to the eyes of men accustomed to see deadly injuries, it had been evident that the chances of the poor Weasel ever coming round were very small.

For hours it was uncertain if the light, which began to flicker after he reached the camp, would go out at once without one flare of consciousness to enable his watching friends to bid him farewell ere he set out on the long march, the end of which no one has returned to tell.

"Will he live, Mackay?" asks the Colonel, coming in for the last time before turning in.

"God alone knows, sir. There has not been the quiver of an eyelid since I first saw him; but for a mirror dimmed now and then I could hardly say he is alive now. There is not a bone broken, as far as I can see, and outwardly there is no wound. The damage is all internal. He may lie as he is for a day or two, but on the third, if he holds on so long, there will be a change one way or other."

"Oh, these boys!" sighs the Chief, as he goes back to his tent very sorrowfully, for he loves them all, mostly, as if they were his sons, perhaps more. "They seem determined to give Charon a chance of a fare."

CHAPTER VI.

"Prepare you, Generals; the enemy comes on in gallant show."
Messenger in Julius Cæsar.

For two days the Weasel's life hangs in the balance, ever inclining from rather than to him, but at the end of the third there come signs of the change which the Doctor had foretold. And after a struggle he recovers consciousness enough to recognize Ian and Charlie, who have been waiting for hours in the hope of seeing him rally at last from the stupor which has too long looked so awfully like death.

"Charlie," he faintly utters, "I killed the brute before he had done for poor Fergus?"

"Yes, my boy, you did. He is only winged. He'll do. We must get you on your legs again, if it were only for old Mac's sake. Are you in pain?"

"None."

"Ah! that's bad — very," soliloquizes the listening Doctor.

"But," he says with difficulty, and after a long pause, during which they fear he is going to sink back into the state of coma which is so alarming, "I think I could drink some 'fizz' if I might have it."

"It's here," says the thoughtful medico, who as soon as he heard his voice, had beaten up an egg in readiness, pouring out a pint of champagne upon it and holding it to his parched lips. "Drink this; it's the best medicine I can give you."

Supported by the others, the Weasel slowly drains the excellent mixture, and sinking back with a look of intense gratitude to them all, the poor little chap turns round and immediately falls into a deep but healthy slumber, to the intense satisfaction of Mackay.

"If that lasts till the morning he will turn the corner, I hope. Go and tell the Colonel, Grant, and ask him to see that there is as little noise as possible in camp. If he can get a good spell of such sleep as that he may live after all."

Throughout the night the kindly Neil watches himself, though he has many volunteers to aid him; but he knows well how little able the best intentioned, if untrained by practice, are to resist the almost overwhelming temptation to sleep in the prolonged silence of the sick-room; and he sees the vital importance of being ready with a restorative the moment the invalid wakes.

"So both your patients are doing well, Mackay?" says the Colonel next morning at breakfast.

"Yes, sir, so far. And as they have been clean livers, which is everything in such cases, they may pull through, though the odds are heavy against them under canvas."

"Ah, you never give yourself credit for all

you can do, Doctor. I thought their case was hopeless when they came in. But try to patch them up, and get them into Bareilly out of this, for we may have hot work which will fill your hands at any moment. Information has just come in that the Nana is in desperate straits for want of food, and will certainly try to break through us."

"Then the sooner we get the cripples away the better," answers the Doctor, rising to go. "By-the-bye, Master, Cameron is worrying to see you. I told him to wait, but he got excited at the suggestion, so perhaps you had better go; but mind you don't talk too much, or his fight for life will be harder yet."

"All right, Mac; I won't be more than half-an-hour."

"Ah, Charlie!" says the sick man feebly, from his charpoy, as he lies on the cool side of the tent; "I am very glad to see you. I was afraid from the way old Neil left me that I should be kept in solitary confinement for some time yet."

"He was a little stiff always about that. Ian and I were coming anyhow."

"I am glad that you came alone; I wanted to have a talk with you. Since I have been lying here with nothing to do but think, my brain seems to get weaker, and I don't see my way very clearly."

"Then don't bother about it just now, Fergus. You are not fit to worry about anything yet, and if it concerns me alone—though I can't conceive what it is—it may well keep till you're better."

"You are very good, but I feel as if I shall be better after I have told you; for though I may get all right, I know these tiger-wounds are apt to turn nasty, and make a mess of one in a hurry."

"There is a solemnity about you this morning which is rather appalling," says Charlie, cheerily, as he draws a cane chair towards the door of the tent. "But if it will do you good to have it out, and it only concerns me, why, fire away."

"That's easier said than done sometimes. I don't know how to begin; for the message is not of my making, and I hardly see what I have to do with it; but I hate mystery, and still more the thought that you evidently don't know it from the proper quarter. Well, it must out," he says, as his listener turns in the chair and wonders if he is off his head. "The truth is, I hear from Olive that her brother Archie is going to marry—Miss—Beauchamp at once."

"What?" shouts Charlie, forgetting Cameron's weakness, his own late pledges, everything but the sense of immediate loss of what was so precious to him—jumping from his chair as if he were shot, and striding towards the stricken man with that in his eye which is a fierce contrast to his placid attitude the moment before.

"Stop!" cries the gigantic Neil, at that moment happily entering the tent. "If this is what you call having a quiet crack with poor Fergus, I must cut your half hour down to thirty seconds."

"Just one minute, Mac. He was telling me—"

"Not another word! Only look at his face, man! And go at once."

"But I must hear—"

"'Deed, Master, but ye're unco' cumstairey this mornen," says the Doctor, losing his temper and his English slightly, as he seizes Charlie by the arm and bundles him out of the tent then and there.

Turning to the invalid, he sees that something out of the common has indeed turned up between them to have excited the one and prostrated the other of two old friends so much at such a time.

In effect poor Fergus is thrown into a state of high fever which fills the Doctor with alarm, and Charlie with remorse for his selfish want of control over himself.

"Is this then the end of his prideful resolution to forget, and seek comfort in the love of one whom the other would least like to replace her?"

Charlie thinks, as he sits alone in his tent and eats his heart out in bitterest vexation at his own weakness.

"Is she still so dear to him that he cannot yet cast her from him, when she has quickly thrown her short-lived pledges to the winds, without one word of regret, hypocritical though it might be, or even the conventional letter of dismissal?

"Is he himself so poor a thing that he does not know his mind? Has he not come hot from fresh protestations of love and truth to another? Does she deserve no better consideration than this vacillating heart-turning, irresistible and impulsive as the light-famished plant to the life-producing sun, because the knowledge of her faithlessness is sealed anew?

"Shall he not rather, since it must be so, feed and force his later passion by the electric substitute he has so timeously discovered?" And he writhes with his self-scourging thoughts as he sees himself both false and weak to each.

Steeped though he is in humiliating self-reproach, suddenly his soldier ear catches the rapid gallop of approaching cavalry, and rushing to the tent-door he sees a party of Sowars dash up, breathless and excited, asking for the "General Sahib."

As he takes them to the Colonel, acting as Brigadier, Charlie learns that these are men sent in by the Commandant of the Punjaub Horse, scouting far in front, who has been nearly cut off by the enemy advancing in force in various directions on the river, evidently pointing for the fords.

In an instant the camp awakes to pregnant action, and all becomes bustle and excitement.

Bugle and trumpet-calls fill the air, while horses, elephants, camels, and baggage-cattle, catching the magnetic enthusiasm at the change from stagnant waiting, join the clamour with shrill neighs and deafening cries of every kind.

In a moment the snow-white tented plain is converted into a mingled mass of canvas, ropes and struggling natives, while the patient beasts of burden kneel and wait for their accustomed loads, some gurgling, muttering, and uttering hideous protests, as is their wont.

Yet in the seeming chaos all is order, and the well-trained troops, with their Eastern aids, quickly show their waiting Chief that they are ready too.

Happily the Colonel is not a man to be caught napping; and, having all in preparation, his orders are sent out by the time the men have fallen in, keen and silent as the weapons by their sides.

"Well, gentlemen, I have not much to add to the orders which will be read to the men presently," says the Colonel to the captains and senior officers assembled round his charger, " but as, I am sorry to say, you will have to act in small detachments in order to hold every ford of the Sarda, and as I can only be in one place at a time, which for the present will be the centre of the line, I have sent for you to say that I hold the officer commanding each post responsible for his part of the river, as shown on the maps in your possession. In a word, the enemy must not break through except over the body of your last man. The odds may, very likely will, be heavy, but I do not think," he adds, with a justly proud smile, as he looks around at the calm, self-reliant men, " that those I see before me have ever stopped to count what might be against them."

Ere they fall in, Ian and Charlie, whose companies, being on the extreme flanks, are to be separated by the whole length of the line of defence, have time to wring each other's hands with the absence of demonstration so characteristic of their order.

"Good-bye, Charlie. I wish we were to be alongside each other this time, and that I had seen more of you lately. It may be that this fight will be my last. If it is, and we don't see the old hills together again, remember me sometimes when you are among them. And— if you will—tell your cousin Julia that if I had got home I would have tried to make her understand why I did not care to woo when I might have done so."

"Don't regret that, Jan, of all things! It's better many times not to have won if you have to lose in the end. There are few things which will bear leaving to themselves, as I have found. If they are light they are blown away beyond reach or recovery; if heavy and worth the venture, some other hand unfettered by scruples will take advantage of the opportunity."

Ere the answering look of sympathy can be further thanked, the pipers sound the gathering, and the two young soldiers, friends from their earliest days, part for the last time.

As the band, standing on the flank, plays, "We'll gang nae mair to yon toun," while each company marches off with its piper to its appointed post up or down the river, the Colonel, who has not got over the teaching of his Gaelic nurse's superstitions, looks after them with a yearning heart and glistening eye, while he mutters to himself:

"I wonder where the blow will fall. I know not which of them I can spare best. I like not the looks of Grant or Macdonald. They are both 'fey,' I fear."

It was a stirring and a martial sight as the Horse Artillery, Highlanders, and Ghoorkas, with the soldier-like and serviceable Sikh Cavalry in front, rear, and flanks, threaded their way through the beautiful glades of the more open jungle to their various stations in the line of defensive posts, now held by picquets of Irregulars.

Probably the enemy had timely notice of the preparations made for their reception, or their plans were disconcerted, for days went by and no attack was made, so that at length a dangerous feeling of lassitude spread among the men as the heat increased in the pestiferous Terai, and even the Ghoorkas, with all their inborn hatred of the Pandy, relaxed somewhat the vigilance of their watch on the foreposts which were entrusted to them.

But at last, as is often the case in military warfare, like that of the elements, the storm broke when it was least expected. And just as the day dawned, the whole line along the Sarda was suddenly and vehemently attacked.

With a generalship which no leader of the rebels had yet shown, with the exception of Tantia Topee, the Ranee of Jhansi, and, perhaps, the Moulvie, each post was forced to show its strength, and was held engaged while the main body of the attacking force was thrown on the flank held by Ian's company, which happily had the additional power of defence afforded by two guns.

With the true instinct of a soldier, and the little scientific knowledge he had picked up under old 'Swinks' at Sandhurst, Ian had employed his time in adding as far as he could to the strength of his position, in the absence of regular entrenching tools, by cutting down the trees in his front, forming *abattis*, and erecting a breastwork with flanks to bear upon the ford. But he had, all told, only eighty of his men besides a company of Ghoorkas and a few artillerymen.

In accordance with invariable custom in the field, the troops had been standing to their arms from an hour before daybreak, so that though the piquets were driven in from the Ghâts somewhat roughly, the Highlanders and gunners were all ready for the attack which developed itself with all the impetuosity shown by Easterns, and, be it added, by some Europeans, when they think they are carrying all before them.

"'Canister,' my lads, at that distance," says the fair-haired young artillery-officer, smelling powder for the first time, but a good deal cooler than when he went up for his first 'exam.' "Give it them as quickly as you can, but steadily, mind, and never let more than one gun be unloaded at once."

While the Ghoorkas are re-forming on the

flanks of the Highlanders, who, to cover as much ground as possible, are extended in single file at intervals, Ian gives his final orders.

Stepping out in front of his men, with his back to the foe, checked for the moment by the crashing *métraille* from the field-pieces, he says in a voice, clear, firm, and calm as if on parade:

"Grenadiers! The Colonel told us off to this post because he knew it was the most likely to be attacked in force. His last words were, 'I rely upon every one of you dying if needs be. The enemy must not break through except over the body of the last man.'

"At Ticonderago, Alexandria, Toulouse, Quatre Bras, those who wore this tartan did not count the odds or the cost. You will do no less, I know.

"There is enough of ammunition to last all day, but do not throw away a round. Not a man is to leave the breastwork until you see me in front again, leading you to charge.

"Piper Macdonald, Seid Suas!"

Taking off their tall feather bonnets, the men placed them on the parapet in the intervals between them, and putting on their Glengarrys achieved the double object of deceiving the enemy as to their numbers and position, while they themselves were less conspicuous.

Decimated by the raking fire from the guns and detained by the *abattis*, the assailants quickly lost the decided *élan* with which they had rushed from the river on the heels of the overthrown outpost, and for a time as the cool, well-directed fire of musketry smote them in front and flank they wavered, but their leader, a magnificent man carrying a small green flag, who seems to be bullet-proof, soon rallies them, and shouting "Deen! Deen!" brings them on again, and with his own hands shows them how to make a breastwork by piling up against the shattered branches the bodies of their fallen comrades.

The attack thus resolves itself into a combat, the result of which is no longer doubtful to Ian, whose only fear had been such a tumultuous rush by overwhelming numbers on his thinly distributed men that he could not stem it.

For hours the fire on both sides continues with the effect that cover and a short distance produce; but the steadier aim and big guns of the defenders maintain a murderous drain upon the numbers that keep on swarming from the river as if determined to advance or die.

Happily no effort is made to outflank the gradually diminishing Highlanders and Ghoorkas, who feel that their only hope of success lies in keeping such a mass at a distance and in their front.

At last there comes a welcome lull, which enables the tired and fasting artillery and infantry to cool their guns and rifles, while their officers cheer the men and look as far as they can to the wounded.

"This is hot work, Simon," says Ian to his only subaltern, as, following the example of the others, they snatch a welcome morsel of food from their havresacks. "I wonder when these fellows will have had enough of it? They seem to take a deal of punishing."

"Because," says the gunner, "the Nepaulese won't have them in the Hills, and they are starving, like rats in an empty granary, in the Terai, so they think they may as well die here and go to their Houris."

"I wonder our people don't send up reinforcements. They must have heard this fire going on all day," says Fraser.

"Ah, they have had their hands pretty full all along the line, I fancy. It has ceased now, but since early morning I have heard heavy firing every now and then," remarks Lanyard.

"You may depend upon the Chief being where it's hottest, and if the weight of the attack is found to lie here he will come as soon as he can; but I should like to beat these fellows off before that," says Ian, as he looks across the open space between them.

Possibly they were waiting for information from the other attacks; but the assault remained unrenewed for some hours, which gave the wearied defenders time to recruit their strength, tried by the continual firing, want of food, and parching thirst, produced by burning powder under a fierce sun.

"They are coming on again," shouts Ian to his sub., "and mean it this time," as he sees them clambering over the now shattered *abattis*. "Keep cool, men! Fix bayonets! If they come near enough let them have the cold steel, but don't leave the entrenchment until you see me leading."

Once more rush the green-turbaned Ghazis to certain death, led by their gallant standard-bearer, as they did at Bareilly, and with a splendid effort reach the parapet in spite of the tremendous fire poured into them.

But all in vain. They are met by men not less determined to win, and to whom death is no more formidable. One after another the foremost of them, though they had gained the crest of the slight earthwork, is brought down, until at last the rest, hopeless of success, fall back. But not before the ghastly wounds of the razor-like tulwar have proved how close and deadly has been the struggle.

"Another rush like that, Simon, and we are done," says Ian, as he looks about and sees his men lying in every direction, while he binds up the young fellow's arm as well as he can. "That's a clean cut you have got. You are lucky not to have had it shred off as completely as poor Gordon's."

"I say! What's that?" cries Fraser, as his pain-stricken face lights up. "I hear the pipers; our fellows are coming on, Ian."

The next minute a round shot ploughs through the flank of the enemy, who have evidently heard the soul-stirring warlike music also, for after a moment's wavering they turn and hastily fall back from the position they have held all day.

"Now, my lads, is our time," cries Ian, drawing his claymore and springing over the parapet. "Prepare to charge. Charge!"—and the splendid remnant of the Grenadiers fling themselves impetuously upon the foe as they retreat towards the Sarda, while the Ghoorkas, drawing their dreaded kukaris, complete the rout.

Alas! that such a day should have such an end, though he would have asked no better.

At the crowning moment of victory in a combat, which for odds and tenacity has not often been surpassed, the gallant Ian, more fleet of foot and lightly armed, attacks alone some sullen matchlockmen—one of whom, stopping suddenly, takes deliberate aim, and, though all too late the next instant a dozen bayonets are quivering in his breast, finds time to fire a Parthian shot through a most noble heart; one of the not least chivalrous of his ever-gallant clan. Alas, for Ian!

CHAPTER VII.

"Ah me, how weak a thing the heart of woman is!"
Portia in Julius Cæsar.

THE results of Lady Alice's strategical advice are not long in showing themselves.

To a naturally sanguine disposition Clarice unites a large capacity for the enjoyment of life; and though at times there come upon her great *accés* of sorrow, when some chord of memory is struck by a sound, a sight, or a perfume—awaking with re-echoing force the diapason of her neglected love-song,—yet Hope, the inevitable sustainer in the heaviest trials, whispers comfort, and she allows herself to float, almost happily, on the daily current of pleasant life, as it sweeps towards the infinite ocean of eternity, at Amat.

As his mother had said, Archie knows pretty well how to accommodate himself to most phases of a woman's heart, if he wishes to win it, and now he feels that it behoves him to lose no opportunity of hastening a *dénouement* which will be irretrievable for Clarice at least, if he does not wish to see the prize, for which he has struggled, risked, and sacrificed so much, torn from his expectant grasp almost at the moment of fruition. For pricking conscience warns him that halting retribution may overtake him at any hour of sleeping over-confidence in his vile scheme.

Too astute a plotter to seem deeply interested in the game, which has virtually become one of wealth and honour on one side, obscurity and infamy on the other, sometimes he misleads his watchful and anxious mother—while even the intuitively more perceptive Clarice finds no cause to shrink from a companionship which, ever-soothing in its pleasantness, has a sweetly subtle flavour flattering to her sorely-wounded pride.

Never allowing himself to appear to seek her

side alone, he, with rare adroitness, is seldom absent from it, until at length, when with high-skilled tact he forces himself away, she finds she has learned to miss the glib and clever thoughts which his fertile brain, from much travel and some reading, is ever culling for her grief-born hunger of amusement.

Lady Alice and her mother, too well content to see the shadows driven from her lately somewhat careworn face, see no danger to her happiness in any passing intercourse. And, while in every sport or pastime, Clarice more or less takes part, Archie grows to closer though unconscious intermingling of her thoughts, less poignant now, of Charlie.

The glinting autumn sun is throwing lengthening shadows up Glen Rua, as some of the younger people from the Castle, having driven up to luncheon at the shieling, are fishing homewards by the river of that ilk.

Famous for its salmon, 'tis rather late in season, a few hours' heavy rain in early morning have put it in rare trim, and the younger ladies have seized the chance of taking lessons in the noble sport from not unpleasant tutors.

To three of them at least the surroundings call up tender memories of a year gone by, in no wise interfering with appreciation of the present; but happily for Archie, they convey no such wholesome antidote to the dangerous poison of his eyes and tongue to Clarice, who, instead of catching trout with them at Craggie, had been listening to the tale she thought so sweet and true—as Charlie told it.

Undesignedly, apparently, Archie takes the lower pools with Clarice as his not unwilling pupil, while Ralph is more taught than teaching by the too seductive Eila. And the other Guardsmen find no unwelcome tasks in showing what an easy thing it is to catch an eager fish, to the not unlearned sisters.

There are few situations more suggestive than that in which "the Beauchamp" finds herself just now.

Alone, but for the gaff and basket-bearing ghillie discreetly lingering behind, with one who not so long ago has openly betrayed his feelings of devotion, which certainly have not yet been quenched, judging by her present experience, Clarice feels her heart beats quicker, as her Mentor, for the moment, leaves the beaten track and they are isolated from the outer world by the ripening hazel-bushes and lichen-covered rocks.

"Now then, Miss Beauchamp," he says at last, when, lightly as the floating thistle-down, she springs to the place he has selected for her first cast—"I think we may fairly take the water home from this. I wish my rod were lighter, but it's from the Shannon, and therefore very pliant. Don't try too long a line, and if you keep your eye on the point you wish to throw your fly to, it will fall not far from it." And he hands her the slender, tapering bit of wood, which to the inexperienced eye looks as if the faintest tug would snap its dainty top.

The perfect calmness of his manner, the intonation of his voice, would be a study for the actor who might wish to learn how to restrain each symptom of a glowing passion, burning for its opportunity, yet to transmit a knowledge of the fact under cover of simulated ice.

She would be less than woman if with her knowledge of his feelings this did not pique her into further trial of his strength. As she takes the implement, so emblematic of her sex's power, their wrists in some way touch in crossing, and for the moment complete the electric circuit. Then the graphic signals which his eyes flash out convince the siren that her power is not less than ever.

And he? For the moment is nearer earthly bliss than he has known for long. In another instant he would have risked the 'No' he feels will come unless he can surprise her with a heart yet more full of active ire against the man who has forgotten her, she thinks. But, with the proverbial instinct of her kind, she has grasped his thought ere it is half formed, and brings him back to safer ground by sober fact.

"Why, Colonel Campbell! Do these fish require no bait?" she asks, as mockingly she holds the flyless casting-line towards him.

Clipped of his wings, he mentally thanks his stars the fall is no greater, and quickly bending on a 'butcher,' he answers, as he hands her back the line: "It would depend upon the sex, I fancy! The finny youth could hardly wish a daintier lure than seeks to bring him to her!"

"I fear he would only appreciate me, if that is what your blank verse means, in a damp unpleasant state which is quite at variance with my present ideas of comfort."

"For heaven's sake take care! Miss Beauchamp," cries Archie the moment after, catching her just in time, as, in her endeavour to cast across, she overbalanced and all but tumbled headlong into the swirling pool.

"Thanks!" she hastily exclaims, as she disengages herself in some confusion from his clasping arms. "I was all but making a more rapidly intimate acquaintance with your typical fish than I intended. It's a dangerous sport, I fear!" she continues blushingly, as she thinks how he has held her.

"Very!" is the most laconic yet emphatic answer, as Archie, flushed and pale by turns, realizes the emphatic truth.

Sitting on the bank, not unnaturally somewhat upset at her narrow escape from at least a ducking, Clarice seeks his face as he stands apart and fastens his dark eyes on hers with an intensity of passion which tells her, mutely indeed but in looks of fire, what she can no longer affect to ignore; and, the knowledge being no longer thrust aside as hateful, he recognizes its reflection in her softened voice and downcast eyes.

"Twice I have to thank you for rescuing me from great danger," she says at last, when the silence has become oppressive beyond endurance. "I trust a third may not come to try you further, for, as you see, I am not good at thanking!"

"God forbid!" he answers on the impulse of the moment; "yet if a wall of fire were round you I would thrust it through to bring you safely out."

The words come from her slowly, almost inaudibly, as if some inner new-born force were uttering, as in brief reply she says, "I believe you."

And then as surging thoughts rise up and make their voices heard, the conflict of the past and present shows itself in ghastly pallor, and impels him into immediate action, come what may.

"Clarice!" he cries, forgetting all his self-restraint.

"Hallo, Archie!" shouts a voice above. "What sport?"

"None, Lord Amat, thanks to this broken top which I am trying to mend," is the ready answer, as he suits the action to the words.

"What a bore! Have you no spare one? We'll drive on and see if Rory has not got another." And, after some laughing commiseration at Clarice's poor chance of winning the gloves for the biggest basket, the drag goes up the Glen.

Archie does not know whether malisons or benisons should follow it from him, as he tries in vain to catch a glimpse of Clarice's averted face.

"How stupid of me!" he says at last.

"Very!" she repeats, in a laughing tone of perfect mimicry, the phrase with which he had answered her before. And, as she turns her face and glances significantly at the fragments in his hand, he sees with glad relief that at least he has not gone too far.

"I am afraid I have spoiled my reputation as an angler."

"For the 'finny youth'!"

"You will forgive me?" he pleads in a tone which thrills to her very heart-strings, as his figure towers above her, and the working of his handsome face exposes the fierce emotions she sees he is controlling in a manner which makes her wonder, woman-like, at all his self-command.

To her deeply-wounded vanity the draught he offers is dangerously intoxicating, but she puts it from her with an inward shudder ere her lips are nigh it; and, as she turns away her face again, she says:

"You must not speak so. You know that I am bound by ties I cannot forget, though—"

"I know, indeed!" he interrupts—"have known, I confess, for long, or I should not have been spell-bound as you have seen. But are there no limits, no mutual obligations in such matters?"

"What do you mean, Colonel Campbell?" she cries, with sudden vehemence—which startles him, but carries with it a subtle consolation in the tone he cannot analyze—as she half starts from her seat.

"Shall I go on now?" he thinks, "or, better still, play yet the waiting game?"

The answer is given by Montie Drummond sounding "the retreat," as the coach drives up again, and, falling back perforce on conventionalities, Archie helps her up the bank.

CHAPTER VIII.

"See, noble Charles! the beacon of our friend, the burning."
Bastard of Orleans.

THAT evening it is little wonder if the minds of the much-chaffed, unsuccessful fishers, hunt in couples over the ground of that disturbing afternoon, and when they say, "Good night," Archie, who has more than once described with elaborate circumstance a fabulous version of the events which have been too really trying for her, receives from Clarice a look, which failing to interpret clearly, gives him infinite cause for thought and sleepless rest.

As he dresses in the morning a sudden inspiration strikes him. By the telegrams in the Scottish papers, arrived the night before, he knows the Indian letters will come in that day. With one of those presentiments which when acted on seem so supernatural, he exclaims, "I will go in and get the bag. Who knows what may be in them?" And even his heart quails as he thinks what may happen if a straight-forward letter of explanation and enquiry from Charlie found its way to Clarice.

The day, turning to drifting rain, as it so often does at that season on the west coast, was not sufficiently tempting for anyone without a purpose to care about the drive to Fort William; so leaving the rest to billiards, smoking, flirting, working, Archie gladly finds himself alone while he hastily looks over the letters.

"The devil!" he exclaims, as he sees those written to his mother and Clarice by Charlie, the morning after he had asked Amy to be his wife.

"Well, truly he does help those who serve him, at times!"—and feeling that he has gone too far to stand still or retrace his steps, he tears them open and reads both.

"He has thrown away his hand, by Jove!" he mutters, as he puts them in his pocket. "Now I must win if I do not blunder; but it is a ticklish game to play. What is this, I wonder, that Master Elliot has to say to the fair Trevor, and his father? I cannot open or destroy them." And in a fever of doubt he tries to steer a middle course.

To let Lady Amat and Clarice have these letters would certainly lead to questions and explanations of which there could be but one end—ruin to himself and his plans—socially and utterly. But to tamper with the others is a step beyond even his elastic conscience. Yet to leave them unread might be to sit on a magazine with a naked candle in it!

The very image braces him, and he draws at once the line over which he will not pass. Some way of escape may offer, but he will go no further on that road.

Such a nice distinction may seem strange, but do we not see it in every phase of life? A man who will charge you one price, yet sell or buy for you at another, is highly esteemed by himself and others, and would resent fiercely any imputation on his probity—as a broker. Another will "stretch a point" to get rid of a flaw in his stable, who would scorn to tell a lie for a fortune? A third would rob a maid, but not a church!—pollute an eternal soul, but respect an earthly tabernacle! Who shall say at what point in his downward course a man may not hesitate?

Having made up his mind, Archie is not long in returning to the Castle, where the letters are duly distributed.

Poor Clarice looks with envious eyes at Eila, whose hasty exclamation tells her that she has heard from Ronald. But as she reads the last few words, Eila drops her hands and groans in bitter sorrow for the blow she sees impending.

"Is it possible," she thinks, "that he can be such a fool?" as she sees, beyond doubt, that Ronald in his postscript plainly says Charlie has just told him of his engagement to Amy. "And without a word to her! It is indeed a strange world! It makes me almost doubt the truth of this!" as she looks with wistful tenderness again at the words so full of hope for herself. "How can I tell her?"

That night she finds she must.

Meanwhile Sir Claude, with the frankness of his joy, tells every one that he has heard from Ronald; and, in the absence of all mention of Charlie or himself, Archie finds such intense relief as may the long bow when the string is loosened. But guilty conscience never sleeps, and in the looks he fancies Eila casts at him he finds fresh food for anxious care.

"Come in!" replies Eila to a knock, which to her imagination speaks itself of sorrow. "Ah, my darling," she cries, as rising from her seat before the fire she thrusts away the already well-worn letter, and welcomes Clarice for their usual midnight conference. "I was just coming with my news to you."

"I could not wait. I saw you had heard from Captain Elliot, and mamma tells me that Sir Claude has a letter from him which conveys enough to show you will be very happy now, my dearest. You remember that I told you so at Christmas?"

"Yes. Indeed you were a kind, as well as most true, prophet. I cannot tell you how happy I am," says Eila, with a brilliant colour and sparkling eyes that do not belie her words. "And yet I cannot be," she adds, while the dew-drops gather quickly, and she turns her face away from the enquiring look, which searches painfully for the truth she feels must now be told.

"Why not?"

"Oh, do not ask me. Why should I have to tell you, Clarice? Why had he not the manliness to speak himself? You did not hear from Captain Grant?" she asks, as a vain hope strikes her.

"No," is the answer, short and cold, as the

word so difficult to say so often is. "That is one reason why I came to you."

"When did you hear from him last?"

"Not since I wrote to him as you suggested."

"Impossible!"

"It's true."

"Heavens! Of what are men made? And he, I thought so true and generous-minded! And you wrote to him?"

"I continued regularly, until the absence of his letters, coupled with what the Campbells told me, made it too clear that there was a misunderstanding I could not solve alone. But I have waited in the certain faith, that if it were possible he could change he would himself be the first to tell me."

"And he has not?"

"No," again answers Clarice, but with a pitifully beseeching look at Eila, which tells her too plainly how her pride and love and confidence are struggling with the desire to know the worst, which her instinct bids her feel is now at hand.

"God forgive him!" exclaims Eila, in a tone which shows she does not, as she puts her arm round Clarice. "Darling! It is not so very long since you told me to be brave. I confess I had then some hope, though perhaps not overmuch. 'Tis now my turn, dearest. And as you are stronger, I will be quick and therefore merciful. I beseech you, do not think him longer worthy of your priceless love, since he can treat it so. Forget him, cast him out of your much too trusting heart, and show him that you have at last awakened from the folly he has himself disowned."

"Eila! Are you crazed? What is it you say? Am I to 'forget,' 'cast out,' the 'folly' of love for him? What do you mean?"

But the poor blanched face and quivering, grief-filled eyes will not answer to the courageous words, and, after one brief silent struggle more, Clarice gives way utterly and weeps the most bitter tears that are ever shed by woman.

With true sympathy and kindliest tact, Eila

sits at her feet and simply strokes her hand, while she lets the expression of her sorrow run its course, terrible as it is from one usually so self-possessed.

At last she whispers: "Clarice, you know what it must have cost me to say what I knew would be such cruel pain to you, what I must think of one who, being the cause of it, can be so forgetful of everything he owes to you as to let such a blow from my hand fall on you. But be yourself, my darling. Think you that, much as I have allowed myself to think of Ron—ald, I would not fling his name, his memory, from me if I thought him so light of love that he could not look into another woman's eyes, were she fair as Helen, fascinating as Circe, without forgetting what was due to me?"

Roused by the words, which touch the keynote of her character, Clarice answers: "You speak as if you had some certain knowledge. I have none. I only know that I loved, he loved, we loved. And we parted vowing we would love for ever. Has all this vanished like a dream? Tell me frankly. And, if you give me honest proof, then I promise you I will do more than cease to wail as if I were a child bereft of its first loved toy."

Pondering for a moment, Eila, with a face that flushes vehemently, then grows deadly pale as she thinks of him who wrote the words and of her who is now to read them, the death-warrant of her present hopes of happiness, suddenly tears the letter from its sweet repose, and laying the postscript before her, shudders while she awaits the collapse she looks for from the needful operation.

Poor Clarice reads, and then convinced indeed, but overtaxed beyond her strength, gazes long and wistfully into space with an expression that tells the direful struggle she is passing through. At last she slowly turns away, and silently leaves the room with faltering steps, in a state of stupor most pitiful to see.

But as the days go by, Eila observes with

mingled feelings that Clarice no longer is the same with Archie. To most there may be little difference in her manner, or the way in which they seem to understand each other, but, with all his undoubted powers of pleasing, he has never been able to blind Eila to the flaws he might so easily have hidden from her had Cupid's glamour come between them. She is not altogether pleased, and Archie reckons her as one against him, little knowing how, on that dreadful night, she had helped his cause by Ronald's letter.

But the revolving wheel of daily life brings its opportunities to those who choose to see, have the power to grasp them. And his most bitter enemy would never have accused Archie of being either blind or timid.

For the benefit of their neighbours, rich and poor, in the way of sport and venison—and the ladies, never averse to such festive days—Lord Amat yearly has one big drive of deer, before the close of stalking.

As the shieling is not expansive enough to

hold all who assemble there for the nights before and after the day which marks the end of summer in the ghillies' minds, the level sward around is covered with marquees.

To the ladies and their maids the lodge is given up, except the rooms devoted to the dance, to which every kilted man, with his particular lass, for miles about is made most welcome.

It has been a truly gala day. Everything has gone well. And even Rory has not a word to say against the behaviour of the deer, the oft-abused ghillies, or the sportsmen's rifles. From earliest morn there had not been a cloud to dim the sun of heaven, or any individual's happiness, so far as known. The torchlight parade of fallen monarchs, who not a day before had flung their royal heads in majestic grace around their gathering harems; the dance kept up till the wearied minstrels failed; the last good nights; the tender hand-clasps; the most expressive looks; the sailing moon; the drifting clouds; the swiftly-following shadows; the moaning, rising wind; the roaring, tumbling fall; the soughing wail of night-flight birds; the many sights, sounds, and memories of that long day, chasing each other in quick succession, have brought at last the ever busy brain of Archie to the verge of sleep, as, restless and overcome with fever-breeding thoughts, he has sought refuge from his tossing bed in the balmy air of night, while she steeps the camp and shieling in blissful rest—when all at once the fork-tongued demon flashes out before him, and, ere he well knows why, instinctively he gives utterance to the fearful cry of "Fire!"

Thrice he has to repeat it as he rushes to the blaze ere the heavy senses of the slumbering are brought to know the coming danger. And then is seen the value of the training born with discipline.

Built, lined, and roofed with pine, high-dried by the summer sun, the lodge is quickly burning, and the awful element leaps in madlike strides towards his sleeping prey before a blow is struck or further sound is made to give them help.

Yet on the instant of alarm Rory is at once himself, and racing like a roe up-hill he reaches what answers to the water-main. Turning on the thousand horse-power of the foaming fall he rushes back, and by the time the half-dressed ghillies are asking what it means he has the engine out and wakes them into action.

The bed-rooms are above those of daily life, and from them come shrieks and cries and calmer questions as the varied inmates ask and learn the meaning of the uproar, and their peril.

Meanwhile the master mind, which sailor-like had foreseen the risk to such a building, has assumed command, and, the others aiding and obeying the orders he so calmly gives, the tumultuous helpless state of frenzy, which at first arose, yields with an inner sense of shame; and many willing hands make all to hope that none may perish.

Ladders are brought, and plaids are held, as

exigency demands, to succour those who are cut off by the dense smoke and heat from the only means of egress. And, without distinction as to order, all are rescued, it is thought, until, as the women standing for a time half-dazed with sudden fright cluster round each other for mutual help and comfort, there comes a sudden cry of "Clarice."

"Where?" shout several voices, but the ring of one surmounts them all, as Archie dashes up a ladder and disappears in blinding flame and smoke.

"Good God, deliver them," is the heartfelt outspoken prayer of those who, looking on, see only death before them. Not so Rory, who with another wetted plaid in hand follows Archie.

It seems impossible that any can stay there yet live. And as the seconds, strained to minutes in the agony, are counted, there falls upon them all a sickening certainty that two gallant men have died besides the fated beauty.

The scorching flames light up with diabolic

glare the nodding pines, the rugged rocks, the fading heaths and the gleaming water, but on the upturned faces it seems as if the king of demons had set his mocking seal, while with horror-stricken eyes they strive to pierce the veil which keeps from them the sight they dare not try to picture.

For all 'tis such a scene as men may well be thankful if they only read of it,—but for the mothers, father, sisters, wife, of Clarice, Archie, Rory, looking on?

Yet we know, our future king himself has proved with characteristic courage, that boldly plunged the naked hand may laugh at molten metal, that the nettle stings not when she is firmly grasped, so Archie, dashing in with the soaking plaid about him, makes straight along the burning passage. In vain he tries to see or hear. All is lurid fire or densest smoke, and, baffled by the overcoming fumes, he falls down on his knees.

And thus he finds by accident the channel

which may save them yet. For there, it's known, exists the only breathing space for life in such a case. And as he creeps along from room to room he is stalked by faithful Rory.

Blinded, almost suffocated, his heart stands still when he sees before him a wall of living flame, which no one but a "fire king" could endure.

"Where can she be?" he signs to Rory, drawing near, who motioning back, guides him to an unnoticed door, which pushing open leads them to the bath-room. And there, prostrate on the floor, unscathed by fire, but senseless from the smoke, lies Clarice.

A plaid tied quickly round the waist makes a rope by which she is lowered, while Rory, lithe and active as a mountain cat, drops nimbly down to catch her. And not too soon, for hardly have they reached the ground ere that, the last of all the Lodge, takes fire.

The cool, fresh air, and some limpid water soon help to show that Clarice is unhurt, and, while the throng in front are in all the agonies of helpless horror, the three so marvellously escaped come walking round before them.

The reaction is too great for many, and for a time strong men as well as women are not masters of themselves.

But soon the prosaic necessities of life happily assert themselves, and the rescued wardrobes are overhauled to put things decently in order. Before long the dawning day brings with it other wants, and hunger claims her due. In a little while, thanks to appropriate clothing, food, and such articles of furniture as have been dragged out, the Castle party, falling unconsciously and quickly into the common-place of daily life, look rather like dissipated votaries suddenly stricken with an odd desire to see the rising sun after an *al fresco* supper.

Suddenly they are startled by the light falling on a gaunt and tattered figure, which, unnoticed hitherto, seems as if it had sprung into life from the heathery knoll on which it stands, and pours out in harsh, sonorous accents, the following medley, in which the words and airs are strangely mixed:

   " Hech, sirs !
What's a' the steer, kimmer, what's a' the steer?
Wha's this wi' voice o' music sweet?. Dinna gang wi' him,
  leddie !
O ! Charlie is me darlin', an' O ! me hert is sair for him.
But dinna ask me gin I lo'e him, sin' Archie cam' to woo.
A Hielan' lad me lo'e was born, but the De'il's rin awa' wi' him.
Here's a health to him far awa' ! But he's a terrible man, John
  Tod !
The last time I cam o'er the muir, she rose an' let him in !
Awa', whigs, awa' ! for I'll drink a health to Charlie.
Bonnie leddie, bonnie leddie, dinna gang wi' him !"

"Who's this lunie, Montie?" mutters Ralph Mostyn, as Archie, biting his lips with vexation, sees the wild-looking old man, bare-headed, with flowing beard and garments, fix his eyes on him, dance up to and round them, snapping his fingers high in the air and shuffling his feet in unison with the weird-like tuneless voice.

"A pet of the district!—a second but inferior edition of Edie Ochiltree—the last of the gaberlunzie, I should think; a lunie, as you say, but not half such a fool as he looks! For Heaven's sake, don't rile him, for he has a tongue like a claymore, if he likes."

"Ha, Grudie! What brings you here?" says Lord Amat, somewhat sternly for him, to the half-witted man. "You were not here last night, were you?" turning sharply round, as an idea flashes across him.

"Na, na, your Lorrdship's a' thegither wrang," he answers, going straight to the thought in a moment. "I hinna bin here langer than th' drinken o' a dram. Th' low o' th' bleeze brocht me here. But," breaking into a jig-like motion, he sings—save the mark!—again:

"The bonnie maister's far awa', at the gruesome Injin wars,
  Fechtin, aye he's fechtin, tho' a's whiles he's may be greetin'.
  Wha's this we hae, this bra' an' sojer callant, smuith an' glib an' fause,
  A' ken the cuckie's plan o' nestin but this lad's birdie's no sae fleetin'."

"That's mine ain, me lorrd; but no sae gran', ye'll be thinken, as Burns, an' the lave o' them. 'Od's but they're aye buzzin in ma heed unco' like a swarmin' skep in a tar-butt. 'Deed," he continues, relapsing into the regular beggar whine, " ye gentry 'll be gaen tae gie us a wheen siller, for the sake o' thae bonnie leddies, as weel as the sang I improveezed," he adds, with an unmistakable thrust out of the corner of his eye at Archie.

" Ay, ay, Grudie! The same old story, I suppose. Whisky and snuff. No home, no food of your own ? "

" Weel, me lorrd, I'll no gainsay yer plaishure. Ye see I hae nae land, nor water, deer, saumon, nor clairet, to distraut me from thochts o' what mecht hae bin."

" Had you spent the price of every glass of whisky you have drunk in your life in buying land, you might have been at least a bonnet laird before this, Grudie. If the land hunger were really as great as the gin or whisky thirst, there would not be so many Radicals or paupers. But there you are, go along and see if there is anything you can have in the larder."

"Mony thaunks, me Lorrd. What's yer wull?" he asks suddenly, turning as he goes by on Ralph, whose question he overheard and has not forgotten.

"I? Nothing!" says the youngster, somewhat taken aback. "But, since you ask me, how did you learn to improvise? From Burns?"

"I?" answers the Gaberlunzie in admirable imitation of the boy's voice and manner, and then relapsing into driest pawkiness.

"Pairtly, sir, and pairtly, no to sae maistly, by minden my ain business!" and he shuffles off, leaving the laughter which follows his retort, a welcome relief to those who have been so tried during the last few hours.

CHAPTER IX.

"Bind up my wounds. My conscience has a thousand several tongues."—*King Richard III.*

BAFFLED in his last spring for life, the human tiger shrank back to the haunts of the not more ferocious beasts of prey, and in their midst the Nana and his blood-stained followers dragged out a miserable existence in the malarious, pestilential, poverty and fever-stricken, jungly swamps, fenced in by enemies on every side, until the retributive Hand had crushed the last wretched defiler of His image.

The combats on the Sarda were the fierce expiring throes of the revolt which had at one time threatened to shake our Indian Empire to its foundation; but it proved, to ourselves as well as to our enemies, that, with all our undeniable faults, we have still the supreme virtues of the conqueror — mighty and overwhelming strength in the hour of trial, calmest justice and tenderest mercy in the day of victory, impartial government in the time of power.

The Red Highlanders had well upheld their traditionary fame and the confidence of their Chief; but, if soldiers ever count the cost, they felt they had bought the last stone of their grand cairn at a heavy price indeed.

With wily skill the enemy had thrown himself with greatest force on either flank, and yet maintained a hold on every post between, so that the hour was late ere the strained strength of Ian's Grenadiers had got their timely help. But in the full tide of conscious victory he fell dead, at the head of those he had led and loved so well. The ties were mutual, and those tough soldiers who knew not fear were not ashamed to weep, as tenderly and reverently they laid him on a gun, and covered him with the flag so dear to all.

Within the last five years many of their best—why is it that it is always the good fellows who go first, must they ever lead the way?—had gone down, and it was no new thing for them to think " the Rag " would add another well-known name to the honoured roll in the memorial window, but never had there been such universal sorrow as for poor Ian.

Kind, gentle, unassuming, like most big men whose hearts are in the proper place, his handsome face and magnificent physique were only a fitting case for such a noble soul. No wonder when his loss was known the whole regiment mourned as for the best of friends. And even Ronald Elliot, popular and well-fitted in every way to take his place as Captain of the Grenadiers, at first was only tolerated as the filler of such a blank.

Charlie and his smart Light Company had their work cut out to hold their own; for the odds were terrible, and the assailants fought as men who know that a lingering death will surely follow if they do not win or die that day. They beat them off, as did all the other posts, but, comparatively early in the fight, Charlie was struck down by a bullet through his chest, which left them little hope, as they laid him gently down against the bank of earth he had thrown up for cover and additional strength.

The wounded were sent into hospital as soon as the day was over, and once again the heart of the kindly Doctor was torn by the sight of the pain and danger he could do so little to relieve.

"We cannot keep them here, sir. At least the recoveries will be few and long. We can surely send them into quarters at Bareilly?"

"Ay; Mackay, we can do no better. God forbid we should lose a single life that may be hoped for; but can they stand the journey?"

"It will try them all, and kill a few, but not so many as the heat and fever of the tents in this malarious place."

And so they went.

To Charlie, suffering from a wound at first pronounced mortal, the news of Ian's death coming suddenly and inadvertently upon him was most trying in the prostrated mental condition he had fallen into since he had heard that Clarice was actually going to marry Archie. Until then her falseness had been intangible, though inexpressibly bitter; but now he could not shut his eyes to the gulf that yawned between them, through his own irrevocable act as well as her faithlessness. He hoped against hope, as we so often do though we know ourselves there is none. And, as he lay in the hot and comfortless dhoolie during the long and weary marches, he strove to comfort himself by thinking that Fergus must have been mistaken, and that when their interrupted interview was renewed he would find it so.

A single-storied, flat-roofed block, white and square, with *porte-cochére* on one side and verandahs round the others, the house that *Rouge ou Noir* has taken is large and comfortable enough to be the temporary hospital their kind hearts have made it.

As you enter from the chicked and shaded portico, a double door-way opens at once on the dining-room, to which the widest of folding-doors gives on the darkened drawing-room. These two rooms, stretching east and west, divide the building. By either side are numerous doors, opening on the sleeping-rooms, to each of which are baths and other comforts, indispensable in an Eastern climate. The openings throughout are *vis-à-vis;* and thus, with the aid of punkahs and thermantidotes, the puckah-house of Bolton Sahib is one of the best of the many pleasant ones which enterprising Bunneahs helped to build as soon as the tumult-raising forces had been driven beyond return.

The large surrounding garden, which owes some of its magnificence to the fostering care of Lola Montes, erstwhile a fleeting glory here, is filled with orange, fig, and almond trees; and surrounded by a tall, sweet-scented hedge of palest green, the purest white, and most brilliant scarlet. In the further corners of its angles stand the stables, kitchens, servants' offices, and, last not least, the luxurious covered swimming-bath.

"Do not give way so, darling!" says Nita, on her knees beside the sobbing Amy. "Thank God, rather, that he is not dead and beyond all hope;"—poor Amy shudders, but her tears are stopped by the kindly, styptic words—"and, if I may say so, that you have the quickly-coming chance of nursing him back to life and strength with your own fair hands. Is not that enough? Come! Let us ride out and meet them in the early morning. If I am not mistaken, he has had no such physic as he will drink from those sweet, soft eyes of yours."

"You were always kind, dear Nita. It seems to me that we two have done but little else than comfort each other, though the account is hardly balanced, for the last half year."

"If the surrounding reeds did not support

each other, how could they live against the current or the storm? I hope and trust this will be only a summer gale, and then your path will be but strewn with the rose-leaves you well may spare. Think of Miss Campbell, still ignorant of the cruel news yet flying to her, and again I say be thankful."

"Ah, yes. I may indeed be that, for at least I shall see him again, but she, poor thing! poor thing! God help her, if her love is like mine."

"He knows best, Amy. It may be that they are both spared yet more cruel sorrow. For I think I would rather see my Terence dead than he were false."

"No fear of that, my darling. Such women as you bind men by cords they cannot loosen, if they would. And now I do not think your *Rouge* could ever turn to *Noir* in any sense."

"Who can tell? Happy as I am and confident, I do not think I should, nor would I advise another to, expose my husband to temptation, the strength of which might be alone computed by the fall."

"And *vice versâ*, Nita. I hope he is not anxious at your tender care of Mr. Fletcher?"

"Dear boy! No; that's impossible. But he is very sweet, and quite repays one for all the fright he has given us. I wonder who he'll marry?"

"So, take care! Those Cupid boys are dangerous playfellows, even for the staidest matrons."

"Nonsense!" says Nita, though her colour raises just the faintest yet most becoming signal. "I have only thought more fearfully of what might happen since Captain Cameron slipped so quickly through our hands."

"Ah, yes; what will Charlie say? Poor fellow! He tried so hard to live, and when he found the die was cast, how quietly he took his fate, and thanked us all for the little we had done. And such heartfelt messages to everybody! Truly Olive had won, has lost, what she will rarely meet again."

Next morning, at the earliest glimmer of the day, Bolton rides with Amy to meet the coming wounded. The cooler air, the springy paces of the high-bred Arab, and the joyous feeling that soon she will see Charlie, combine to bring a rosy flush of colour to her pale, soft cheek; and, as her tall slight figure is set off by the French-grey habit, so becoming to the blonde, her escort thinks the Highlander is indeed a lucky fellow to have a nurse so fair and anxious.

A steady gallop, after they have passed the town, takes them swinging out the road to Peeleebeet, until at length the dhoolies come in sight. At the first glimpse of the long, low, blood-coloured, most suggestive-looking litters, poor Amy's heart falters, and, pulling up, she begs Bolton to go on and tell Charlie she is there, for she has not strength to see him suddenly. It is well she did, for when at last he finds his bearers out, the surgeon by his side whispers that his life hangs by a hair, and that he cannot answer for the consequences if he is wakened from the sleep which may end in death, but possibly with returning life.

With greater tact and delicacy than many would give him credit for, Bolton canters back, and suggests their hurrying home to have everything in readiness. Amy, rather dreading what she has been looking forward to so much, not unwillingly consents, and by the time the litter is resting in the portico, she rejoices that the pleasure of their meeting is yet to come.

Poor soul! As the pallid, wasted wreck of the gay and handsome soldier is lifted in, it needs all the self-command at her disposal to suppress a shriek of horror. But the Doctor's warning glance helps her restraint, and she soon inspires him with confidence enough to be installed as nurse in chief.

For days the vivifying forces struggle hard with death, who nightly seems to creep yet nearer to the object of so much love, and it may be truly said that if Amy had not cherished every spark of life, the flickering flame could not have stood against the drafts which seemed to come with such persistency, that no one else maintained the hope she would not bid farewell to.

At last her strength, and care, and faith meet with their due reward. After a night of such quiet slumber as he had not known since wounded, she hears his sentient voice; and, creeping to his side, her heart is filled with grateful joy in feeling that the crisis of his present fate is passed, and that he owes it most to her.

"Now, dear lady, I must send you off, or I shall have you on my hands also," says honest-hearted Neil. "No; do not speak. You can see he knows you are not going far away—and that rest is needful for you. Besides," he adds, with careful purpose, "I want you to be fit enough to look after him on the homeward journey, which you must both make as soon as he can move."

"Oh! How soon?"

"I cannot say! But I promise you not an hour later than can be helped. You will have Mr. Fletcher too, for he is not fit to stand another hot season, and, as a healthy reliable one in case of need, Captain Elliot must make his plans fit in with yours."

These words, which Charlie drinks in with the feverish desire of the invalid abroad, are worth all the drugs in the pharmacopœia, as Mackay well knows, and from that hour his recovery is marvellous to those who do not understand the attractive powers at work.

But though he daily gathers strength, his mind seems ever absent or on the stretch, and those about him see and wonder at the change from his former happy manner to the grave silence with which he listens to the attempts to cheer him up.

"This won't do, Fletcher," at length the Doctor says. "If we can't rouse him from this lethargy he'll never leave Bareilly, far less India. Go in and knock this blue devil off his chest somehow. It's killing him by inches. Find out what is on his mind, for that alone is now diseased."

"All right, Mac. I'll do what I can, but you know the Master is not to be driven against his will."

Next evening, after his last visit for the day, he takes the Weasel aside and says, "Well?"

"It is by no means 'well.' I wish it were. As I feared, it was a deuced nasty thing to do. At first I thought I would try poor Fergus."

"Ah, I remember they had some words; at least not quite that perhaps, but the last time they met I found Grant rating at him like—"

"Yes. I know. But though it will be a long time before he gets over his and Ian's death, it is not that. Poor Fergus explained all that to me. So then I spoke of Mrs. Gardenne and our going home. And out came the mischief with a rush!"

"Do you mean—?"

"I mean nothing, most sagacious Esculapius,

but I think there is a devil of a game of cross purposes somewhere, which can only be ended by getting him away home, but then assuredly in someone coming to grief. My advice is to trouble him and ourselves as little as possible, but make tracks the moment we can."

"So be it! One way or other, I fear we'll never see him again with us. 'Od! but it has been a wearifu' job this mutiny, from first to last," says Neil, as he thinks of those that have gone down in it.

The last night comes at length, unexpectedly, quickly, as it often does when long looked for, and the Nainee Tal friends sit together once more with hearts which tell their fulness by their silence.

Charlie alone is more like what he once was than any of the others, and poor Amy, now accustomed to the varying whims which she attributes to the invalid's sick fancies, is happier than she has been since he came in so nigh to death.

"Ah, Mrs. Bolton, if we could but take you

and *Rouge ou Noir* with us, I should have nothing left to wish for," says the sentimental Weasel, as they walk outside to catch the welcome evening air.

"It's very pretty of you to say so! But, alas! I see no hope of my leaving this for years. By that time our days of fun and trial out here will have faded from your memory, I fear; and, if we meet, you may put up your glass and say: 'I knew you there, and will again should ever I go back.'"

"Don't say such things, even in joke!" impulsively pleads the Weasel, whose sensitive little heart has been touched by her far more than either of them may know, though each may guess not widely of the mark. "You cannot mean you think I shall ever forget all you have been, what you always must be, to me. Do I not owe to you my life, whatever that may be worth without you?"—and, moved by the impulsive feelings of the moment, he carries the hand he has seized to his lips.

"Don't be ridiculous!" she answers, as she withdraws it quietly, though there is a dewy softness in the eye and a quavering in the voice which belie the words. "You are all so mixed up in the happiness I have found since that day on Cheenee that I confess I feel very tenderly towards you. But don't be stupid," she hurriedly adds, "and go away dreaming that you or I care for each other more than we ought. You are very dear to me, have been since you showed how little you thought of yourself in saving Terence, and I hope you will not forget me—quite! But draw the line at that!" And as she turns to join the others she gives him her hand again, which he kisses once more; but in a way which tells her that she has timely pruned the wildly-growing briar into an honest stock, on which the truest friendship for herself may bud and blossom without injury to the rose she feels, with half a sigh, will come and take its rightful place hereafter.

"You will find it rather hot, Elliot," says

Bolton, as they are left to smoke alone, "in those confounded *dak gharries*. I would always rather travel on a mail-cart. One does get some air on them."

"And sun!"

"Not to hurt at the pace you go. But at night you may come to greater grief."

"How?"

"I was coming up from Bombay once in a hurry; and the Bheels took it into their heads that I was worth robbing, I suppose. Anyhow, as we were going along as only those ponies can go sometimes, I found myself suddenly flying through the air, and then—there was a blank. When I came to myself, feeling rather cold, I found I was nude as the day I was born, the mail-driver with his throat cut from ear to ear, the cart upside down, and the pony with its knees like a pair of Evan's kidneys. I fancy I was not worth killing twice over for the small amount of loot they got, or I should not have been left to tell this traveller's tale. As it was

I nearly broke my neck by tumbling into a nullah at the side of the road in crossing the rope which, tied from tree to tree, had brought us down. The trudge I had into Mhow, bare-headed, bare-footed, bare everywhere, and the consternation I created when I appeared crossing the parade in the uniform of 'the Buffs,' you can imagine.

"The gharrie is like the homely 'growler,' safer if slower. So I hope you will have a pleasant journey. But you will find it hot; my eyes, how hot, in the Red Sea!"

"Listen to him, Weasel!" says Paul to Fletcher, who has just joined them, "as if he wouldn't sit on a gridiron all the way, if he could only go with us."

"I believe you, my boy. But all the same, I would rather avoid that same bit of water at this time of year."

Nita and her Terence are sitting alone at breakfast, *triste* as the best-matched pairs must be after suddenly losing several pleasant guests whose lives have for some time been intertwined with theirs.

The letters and papers are brought in, and are doubly welcomed when she sees one is from Amy.

Presently, looking up from his *Englishman*, Bolton says: "I hope she has given you an amusing *screed*. She must have had a fine time of it, going down country with those young fellows to look after her!"

"Yes. She writes from her late husband's sister's house, and says she can never forget the pleasant gipsy sort of life they had, and wishes it had lasted longer. Why! What's this postscript? 'Charlie has just been here. We must sail to-morrow in the 'Kandy.' All is changed. I can't write more now, but you shall have a budget from home.' What can have happened, I wonder?"

"Happened? Why he has married her! Not surprising she had no more time for writing!"

"Married!" cries Nita, jumping up and seizing

the paper from him. "Let me see! Oh, there can be no doubt!" as she reads the published list of passengers. "But why could she not say so? I am so glad, Terry, ain't you?"

"Well, yes; if it pleases you, dear. But there seemed to be always something on his mind that I didn't like, for one. He gave me the impression, especially since he came here, of not caring half as much about her as she deserves, which is blanked ungrateful of him, to say the least of it."

"Terence! You surprise me!" says Nita, in a serio-comic tone, to cover her own vexation at his perceptions agreeing so closely with her own. "What do you mean?"

"I mean that he don't like her half as much as—I do you, *par exemple!*"

"Ah! but he is a cold Scot, you must remember, not a fiery Irishman like you!"

"Bedad! If it's compliments that we're goin' to pay each other, be aisy, or I'll make myself black again in a jiffey."

"And you promised me that awful day that you would never dye again!"

"Did I now? Ach! I was foolish thin; for I must die wance more annyhow!"

"You may say what you like, this morning. *Rouge gagne! Le jeu est fait!*"

CHAPTER X.

" And I could weep, would weeping do me good."
The Queen, Richard III.

THOUGH the excitement of the moment kept them up for the time, the reaction of all the ladies after the fire at the shieling was sufficient to make them most thankful to find themselves comfortably at the Castle again. And for some days Archie saw no more of Clarice, whose nervous system had received a severe shock, though happily not a burn or scratch was there to mar her beauty.

The intervening time afforded ample opportunity for thought to both; and, truly, if he had packed the cards he could not have brought about a happier shuffling for his hand.

"Undoubtedly he loves me, has loved me, he says, for long. He is no false, light-hearted one to give, and take, and throw away. Three times he has saved my life, and, as he said he would, has rushed through living fire for me. Can I refuse him what he wants so much, what is so little prized elsewhere? Ah, me!" And Clarice, as she thinks how proudly sure she had been of Charlie, weeps again and again, from mingled grief and shame at the wealth of love she had so freely given being hurled back without one word.

"I must go to-morrow, Miss Beauchamp," says Archie, as they stroll through one of the conservatories the morning of her reappearance. Is it the simple words, or the manner of their utterance, that makes her start, imperceptibly almost, but enough to make her keen observer's heart bound with the anticipation of coming triumph? "I began to fear I should have to leave without being able to assure myself that you are really none the worse." But his eyes—as they wander from her fair and wavy hair, coiled like a diadem about her queenly head, to the classic purity of her Grecian face, contrasting in its ivory smoothness so harmoniously with the exquisitely fitting dress of maroon-coloured velvet, which shows in every line and fold the wondrous symmetry of her matchless figure it will not be so envious as to hide—tell her that he sees no flaw in her, and bring up the faintest tinge of warmth which, connoisseur as he is, is all that he thought wanting to complete the picture of her perfect beauty.

With all her apparent coldness, Clarice has her impulsive moments. On the instant she puts out her hand with more than gratitude in her eyes, and the soul-felt thanks, which stir her heart beyond control, flash out from the dark-lashed violet orbs, which for the moment stand unveiled, as they have never been to him before.

Breathless, speechless, from the spell they cast upon him, Archie takes the slender hand, and ere he well knows how his lips are pressed ecstatically upon it. And yet it is not withdrawn. May he venture further now? "Why not?" hope whispers; and drawing nearer, as his eager eyes passionately seek hers, now turned away with tantalizing coyness, he whispers in the hoarseness of his agitation, "My own at last."

There is not a word to guide him; but she does not increase the narrow space between them, and when at length, grown bolder by the answering silence, he steals his arm around her the nascent love leaps from her upturned half-closed eyes, and he drains it to the full, as ardently beyond all words he strains her to his breast, smothering her with rapturous embraces.

Too eager in his conquest, he does not notice that there is no response. "*Il y a toujours l'un qui baise, et l'autre qui tend la joue*"—and his French experience may have reconciled him to the fact. At least he is satisfied.

And she? Who knows the heart of woman? Does the mourner for the "dear departed" always mourn? What comparisons arise to many, as the present and the past stand side by side together in the mental window? To the veriest *ingénue*, as she lets the doting lover gather sweetest honey, are there no experiences, discreetly veiled, to raise a mocking finger?

After all, in any case possession is a cardinal point, as lawyers tell you, and Archie, for the present, is too well content to conjure up a corroding acid.

Extricating herself at length, with deep and most becoming blushes, silent and with downcast eyes, Clarice smoothes her somewhat ruffled plumage, but helps him not a word. Not easily abashed, the practised Guardsman is rather disconcerted. Further advance he cannot make. Retreat is clearly futile. And yet, if silence be golden, why should he complain, since at least he is not rebuked?

To the attack belongs a moral strength which often turns the evenly-balanced scale. And with wise audacity Archie at last says, " I could not help it, Clarice; you should not have tempted me beyond my strength!"

"I had not thought you were so weak, I must confess!" she answers, with some prudery; "but, if I did, forgive me! I think neither of us remember all we ought; I daresay it is all my fault. But I must be frank, lest you reproach me more hereafter!"

"That is not possible, my——"

"Stop! For one minute let me speak, and then——"

"Rather be silent, if you will, for ever than take away the hopes you have allowed to grow unchecked."

"Ah! yes. It is there I have been so wrong. You know I was engaged to—to—Char—to Captain Grant? Well,"—as he is constrained to bow in acquiescence,—"I must confess to you, that if he had been true I should never have thought of change." Again he bends his head. "Yet more; that for long I could not bear you, and that even now my regard—I cannot call it by a warmer name—is a tardy second growth which owes its life to anything but love. Can you be content with that?" she asks with a defiant tone, which makes him long to clasp her in his arms again, and then cry, "Yes, as long as you are mine, not his."

Yet his eyes flash, and he bites his lips with a sense of pain as he thinks of all he craves for, gives, and is like to get.

"I am well content, if you will let me win you, as I said. I will wait until I warm the ashes that you speak of with such fire as has been burning here since I first saw you."

"So long ago as that?" she asks, as her eyes wander over his Velasquez face, the tall well-knit figure, and she thinks, "This is no new lover then!—but only tardier. Is he more true?"—and the suggestive question makes her shiver with a new-born fear. "Are all men false? Will this be like the last, or worse perhaps?"

Ah! once a truly trustful heart is smitten by a graceless hand, it is long, if ever, before the wound is healed.

"Yes; I was on guard when you were presented. And as you swept by, the fairest *débutante* of that or any other season since, I vowed, though I did not even know your name, that you alone should be my wife."

"That was rather bold! But you are so, I have heard, where dangers are more material; and as I have proved indeed myself. Oh! why should I hesitate to thank you as you will, when if you had been otherwise I should be already less than nothing?" And turning impulsively towards him she holds out both her hands, which taking, he folds her to his heart yet more warmly than before.

"And now," she asks; "you are going to-morrow? Let me say, then, but one thing more, frankly; my widowhood, I can call it nothing else, began when Eila Trevor told me he was engaged to Amy. It must endure a year. During that time I will try to learn to give you a better return for your love; and then, if you are still of the same mind——"

"Do you doubt it?" he interrupts. "But you do not mean to send me away till then?"

"No. I shall have to con my lesson now and then, or I should never master it! Come and see us sometimes. We shall be in Clayshire all the winter, more or less."

As time went on the wound, untouched, began to heal. For Mrs. Beauchamp, with true tact seeing that it was beyond her art, left well alone; while Lady Amat, wrapped in sorrow at her son's misguided conduct and continued silence, which she attributed to shame, knew she would only make the burden greater for poor Clarice by trying to share it with her.

Hunting, dancing, laughing, as the world goes, the year rolled by, and another is growing fast when London sees again the season coming on, as Lenten fasts are over. Half Archie's probationary time is gone. He has not failed to give Clarice every opportunity of studying such passages of love as he can lay before her, and on the whole he has no reason to complain, though at times he is tempted to wonder if Charlie's caprice was due to coldness on her side.

"Well, Archie, and how do you get on?" asks his mother one afternoon when he happens to look in and finds the trio all alone. "I think you are hardly wise, looking to the past, to let such a whimsical young lady have too much time. She may change her mind again. Why did you not clench the matter when you had the chance at Amat? Cold iron is not easily bent to will."

"I fear I was rather premature in telling Fergus you were to be married immediately, as I thought of course you would when at last you had got her to say 'Yes.'"

"My dear Olive, you are too impulsive. The days of Lochinvar are over. On the whole, I fancied I had not done so badly; and, though I confess I should like to have things more settled, I do not see how I can force the pace. You know as well as I do how impossible that is when one has to ride a waiting race."

"You know best, of course," she answers; "but, as mamma says, one never can tell how quickly things may alter, and you have already sacrificed enough, I think, to the manes of her first engagement. Possibly she is only waiting for a little gentle pressure to relax. Try her."

"You women read each other well," is Archie's somewhat sneering answer. "But you may be right. I will try to-morrow."

Ah! 'to-morrow.' How many hate the word, with much reason?

Hardly has he entered the Club when he meets Gilbert Elliot with an expression on his face which tells him there is something coming he will not like to hear.

"Heard the news, Archie?" The tone is kindly, sympathetic.

"No. What? I have just come in."

"Those Highlanders have been at it again; they seem to live, or rather die, poor chaps, too freely, on brimstone without the treacle—unless it comes in honours posthumous. But this is serious for your people, old fellow."

"What is it?" is the impatient answer, for though Elliot's manner is very different from his usually *insouciant* air, Archie is on the rack, and his mind conjectures all sorts of probabilities.

"They seem to have had it pretty well to themselves, for there are few other names mentioned; but I am sorry to tell you that your sister will have an awful shock."

"What! Fergus Cameron?"

"Yes; he is reported dead, simply. Ian Macdonald, killed in action. Chalie Grant, dangerously wounded, shot through the lungs; and several others."

"Good God! I have only now come from my mother's. It will be terrible news for them all."

"I feared so. There is one advantage in their sex. They don't belong to a club, so they are not likely to hear it until you go up; but I would go quickly lest any one blurts it out to-night somewhere."

"Thanks, Gibbie. I will go at once," and he does.

"Devilish odd," mutters Elliot, as he sees him jump into a hansom. "He don't seem to think twice of Charlie. Perhaps I should not either, under the circumstances," he adds *sotto voce*, as he remembers what he has heard lately at odd times. For it is hard to keep things hermetically sealed if exposed to that sharpest of all weapons, the world's tongue. "What effect will this have, I wonder, on his little game? Poor Charlie! He seems to have got it pretty hot all round ever since he went to that outlandish country."

"I say, Gilbert; have you seen Amat this afternoon by chance?" asks a voice in a disturbed tone, which he recognizes before turning round as that of the General, after he has heard the news.

"Yes, sir. I saw him go into the Carlton not ten minutes ago."

"Poor fellow! It is hard on him to have these repeated blows. I fear it will try her very much. I suppose you know nothing more than is posted up in the room there?"

"No. I have just seen Archie Campbell, who had not heard a word until I told him, and he went off at once to break it to his people."

"That's right. Poor Fergus! Poor Ian! Few, if any, better wore a belt. But I must try to see Amat before going home. Addio!"

"By Jove! There will be some sore hearts presently. How will Clarice stand it after all? She must have liked him not a century ago! Thank God, Ronnie is out of it, so far, well!" and he goes off to see the Trevors.

"Oh, I am glad to see you, Gilbert!" cries Eila, as he finds her alone. "Papa rushed in here a few minutes ago from 'the Rag,' full of the awful news which he heard there; and he has gone to tell the servants in Wilton Place not to let the Campbells see a paper, or anyone, before Archie goes, as of course he will do when he hears. What a terrible blow it will be for Olive! But I am not sure that poor Clarice is not almost as much to be pitied. Oh, it is too dreadful, altogether!" and the excited girl, burying her face in her hands, sobs hysterically.

"Don't give way so, Eila!" says Elliot, gently. "Ronnie is all right this time, and from what they say I fancy the fighting is over now. If so we will see him home before long."

"Yes, I know. My anxiety is not entirely selfish. I was thinking of those poor Campbells and the Amats. I don't know how Charlie's mother will stand up against it, for she has been very feeble all winter. As to Clarice, I confess I am afraid to go and see her, until she sends for me."

"Shall I call there and leave a message for you?"

"How kind! Yes—stay! I'll write, and if you will leave it I shall be so grateful."

"Truly," thinks Gilbert, after he has been and heard the distressing state produced at all three houses, "this should be a solemn warning to Venus. Mars is ever a dangerous god. But they all do it, bless them! And then the time comes when they have to pay for the pleasure. It is a very old story, yet they don't seem to grow much wiser."

The Zulu monarch who would not allow his warriors to philander was not far wrong, in theory.

On Olive, impulsive and demonstrative, the effect was appalling, and at first it seemed as if reason had left her. With no deep-seated strength or higher feelings to rely upon or guide her, the poor weak mind tottered, and for days it seemed as if her one incessant cry of "Fergus! oh, my Fergus! Come back! come back to me!" must end in lunacy, if not death. Happily when nature spends her strength, either by short and violent hurricanes, or more prolonged if less furious gales, there comes recuperative calm. So at last the anxious mother and her sister were thankful enough to see her weep the gentle tears of rational grief, from which in time the shallow nature, as the tide receded, came back to smoother sorrow, rippling sadness, and finally to normal, placid stillness, reflecting only self.

To Julia, the stronger, more self-contained character, the double shock of Charlie's danger, and the death of Ian, whom she found she had grown to like better than she knew, was one of those rare blessings which come to us in shape of sorest trials. When she emerged from it she was a better woman, with greater chance of happiness than if either of the schemes for it had yielded what she hoped for.

But, as Eila knew, for Clarice the burden was the most intolerable, for she had with her own hands cut away the right to think of and lament the dangerous state of Charlie, and none saw clearer how heavily the chances were against him now.

Some days elapsed ere she could respond to Eila's note. At length she answered it in person.

"Oh, darling!" she cried, "I cannot bear this any longer. I must tell you all I feel, or my brain will burst. I feel that all this sorrow is a sort of judgment on me. How, or why, I know not; but I am sure I deserve it. And I am going to write and tell him that all must be at an end between us."

"My dearest Clarice, I am so glad you have come at last! But do be calm! Who are you going to write to? Why should you reproach yourself with what might equally have befallen Ronald? And what has that to do with your prospects of happiness?"

"Oh, Eila! I have none. I am utterly miserable. I have been weak, vain, proud, unforgiving, hasty, anything and everything, but—*au fond*—not forgetful. And now I find I cannot, come what may, cast out my love for Charlie. He may forget me, he may love any other if he will, but I cannot—will not."

"My poor darling!" exclaims Eila, with intensest pity, as she takes her in her arms and tries to soothe her. "This is better late than never, but very terrible—not only for you, but for Colonel Campbell, whom you certainly have for some time led to believe you will marry."

"I know! It is quite awful! But I cannot, simply—what am I to do?"

"Hum! May I see him? He don't like me much, I know. Perhaps that is as well just now! For the moment I can see nothing for it but temporizing. May I try what I can do?"

"Yes, certainly; anything. Only don't let me ever see him again!"

Next morning Archie is surprised by a note from Eila, asking him to come to luncheon; after which, having confided her plans to her gladly-consenting father, she goes straight at what she feels to be the biggest fence she has ever looked at, without stopping further to measure it.

"Colonel Campbell, I daresay you were surprised by my note this morning? It was very good of you to come, for I don't know how else I could have managed to convey to you a very unpleasant matter."

Archie bows, mechanically and somewhat stiffly, drawing himself up in his chair as if to meet a coming blow.

"You are engaged to my dearest and oldest friend?"

Again he bows; but no light has yet dawned upon him, and he remains politely attentive still.

"She came here in the greatest distress yesterday. You can imagine, of course, how the dangerous state of one who was so dear to her as Captain Grant must have upset her?"

"Why don't she come to the point at once?" thinks Archie, as he bows again. "I shall become a sort of nodding mandarin presently."

"Well; I am sorry, for your sake, to say that she has arrived at the conviction that her feelings of regard for him are still so strong that she cannot keep to the engagement she so inconsiderately entered into with you."

"Miss Trevor!" loudly exclaims Archie, losing immediately all his apparent *sang froid*, and springing to his feet.

"Stay, Colonel Campbell! It is not necessary to get excited. You had better hear me out calmly. Sit down. I sha'n't detain you much longer. I am now acting by her express wish and authority, which you may easily verify, if you like, after this interview is over. Believe me, although I tell you frankly I was surprised by and disliked your engagement, I reasoned with her and pointed out that you have been too long led to believe that she would fulfil it. It was useless. She said, in effect, that she still likes Captain Grant too much for her own happiness, or yours, to marry you—that it is better to avow this now than later. And she consented to my seeing you on one condition."

"That was?" he asks eagerly, and his agitation is so great that even Eila's dislike to him cannot prevent a twinge of regret for his blighted hopes.

"Shall I use her very words?"

"Yes," he snaps out, but it is with the air of the ravenous leopard waiting for his long-delayed bone.

"They are cruelly hard, but it may be better so. They were: 'Don't let me ever see him again!'"

Strong man as he is, the blow is so unexpectedly great, as the probable consequences flash before him, that he staggers back on the seat from which he had hastily risen to hear her last sentence, and for a moment he is so ghastly pale that Eila thinks he must collapse. At last he gasps out:

"Can you, will you, give me no hope, then? You do not know how dear she is to me!" And the proud, passionate man shakes like a child with the emotions he will not further show.

Eila has never so nearly liked—certainly she pities—him, as she says, "It would be a cruel kindness to bid you hope. I do not think there is the slightest shadow of it for you just now; but if you will promise faithfully to leave her alone until I can tell you that I believe you may come back with a chance of success, then I will pledge myself to do so, coûte que coûte."

"Agreed! I trust you, Miss Trevor."

"You may. And I rely upon your honour?"

"Certainly."

That night poor Clarice sleeps more happily than she has done for months; and Eila loses no time in telling Lady Amat what makes that sad heart lighter than it has been of late.

The succeeding mail brings in a cheery letter from the Weazel, giving a fair account of Charlie, never mentioning Amy, and saying that as soon as they can manage it, he and Ronald Elliot are going to come home with him.

Once more the veil of sorrow seems to rise and let the light of hope come in. At intervals Lord Amat hears from Fletcher, who seems to have become a rare amanuensis, until at length there come a few brief lines from Charlie himself—the first for long, saying that in three days he hopes to embark in the 'Kandy,' and, all well, to be with them shortly after this note has reached them.

As they look at the well-loved writing, and see how weakness has disfigured its fair, bold character; as they think of what he has gone through, and how soon he is to be with them, all their sorrow and vexation seem to fly like malarious mists before the rising sun; and in her joy forgetting all but happy possibilities, Clarice, freed from the incubus of Archie, who she hears has gone abroad, joins them as of old, while they almost count the hours until they shall see their dear one back again.

Alas! as if their cup of sorrowful anxiety had not been nearly filled before, the trial of their strength comes more crushingly than ever, no kindly, thoughtful War Office intervening this time. One morning as they sit at breakfast in the bright and happy-looking sunlight, Lord Amat, taking up the *Times* and glancing through its columns, reads, in type which catch the eye and scorch the brain of those whose hearts are riven, " Loss of the ' Kandy,' with all on board."

CHAPTER XI.

"That death's unnatural that kills for loving."—*Desdemona*.

MAN is not born to live alone, nor woman either; especially when she loves, as Adéle. The very nature which impelled her to throw her heart, grand in its passions, truth, and faith, at Archie's feet gave her likewise that which casteth out all fear; and, after he had brought her back to France, leaving her again with the fondest protestations, she waited; as we all have done at times, with a listening, straining ear for the footsteps of the one whose lightest promise is more valued than the vows of the whole world beside. So she lived.

Have you ever robbed a mountain-top, and brought away its wildest, but most beauteous plant, to gratify your eye and please a passing whim? And when the fancy is past, or other cares have interposed, has your conscience struck you for the deed which killed the life that looked to you for but a little gentle thought?

Never strong, as are the hardier daughters of the North, the somewhat fragile Adéle had carried back with her the seeds of death. Yet it needed but a loving careful hand to heed their growth, and that she lacked. In vain she waited patiently, most faithfully. No reproach was cast; and, obedient as the loving spaniel, she kissed the scourger of his silence in her trusting loyalty.

As he let the hour-glass run, did he not see the glittering specks which might warn him ere it were too late? Blinded, by the too near presence of the goddess he was worshipping, he did not; and she, poor child, fearful lest she might break the silver cord, waited—and in the waiting dreamt.

Who have such visions as the loving? Is not

every leaf, the veriest pebble by and on the path, a record of the past—a promise of the future?

"'Twas there we met! 'Twas here we parted. No; not there, for here it was he vowed he'd come again. Is not such the burden of the song?"

Does not the running stream itself re-echo every word? Do not the breezes whisper back the refrain of the well-remembered tale? Ah me!—if the heart beats quick, turns sick and faint, if she, or he, for whom we wait be but the flickering of an eyelid late, what must Adéle have felt as the months rolled on and yet he never came?

The Trianon has much to answer for, yet its trim and ancient precincts had never listened to a sweeter, truer voice than that which warbled while she had wandered with him there. "You love me, Louis! You will not stay so long away? You will think of me counting the hours until I know you are flying back? Ah! how can I live without you after this too brief happiness? Tell me again, *mon cœur*, you will not forget that without your presence I must die. The purslane is not more dependent on the love of Phœbus than I on yours. I am better, stronger when you are with me, but there are times, when you are from me, that I am almost stifled by a fear, and I tremble lest I go away for ever without one more last fond look of you. Oh! whatever happens, promise that you will not let me leave the world I love for your dear sake, alone?"

The touching voice, the pleading eyes, the trembling limbs, while she clung to him as does the fragile, graceful tendril to the hard and heartless forest tree, came now too late, alas!—for even then his heart was panting for the calm, cold beauty, whose very iciness had fired him far beyond the lavish passion of the one who had counted all things gained since they were lost for him.

Yet, dissembler ever, he simulates too well. And, as he clasps her to his heart, he vows anew that ere the autumn leaves have fallen he will return to leave again no more.

At first the days were counted, then the weeks. Was it months since he had gone, and yet he had not come? Forbidden by his solemn adjuration, she dared not write. At times a letter came from him, but it seemed to her impulsive heart as if the Polar wind had breathed upon the paper and quenched the fire she looked for all in vain. But as the golden russet feathers of the forest's mighty wings were plucked by winter's ruthless hand, and fluttered to the cold hard earth, she watched their eddying fall, and shuddered as she wondered if she too would sink thus noiselessly and unheeded, to be swept away and lost amidst the growth of newer things.

Too proud to express the doubts, or, even to herself, do more than vaguely admit the fears his silence forced upon her, Adéle suffered mental tortures which exceeded far the pain her shattered frame endured.

Stung at last by shame a great deal more

than love, Archie wrote to try and palliate his inability to do even a part of what he had promised. With the quick perception of true love she tore the veil aside, yet not in anger, for she said: "If I could only see him, his love would live and so might I. I will write but once and tell him. Surely he will come. He cannot know."

And then she waited hopefully. But when Fortune turns away her face she casts no backward looks. To catch her eye she must be met. She is very hard to overtake. Thus, as poor Adéle's most touching letter reached him, he was steeped to the lips in all the flattering hopes which followed the recurring visits down to Clayshire in the winter.

"*In vino veritas.*" Success is no falser test. Show us the man who will bear it as we think well, and we speak more truly highly of him than if he battled hard with adverse fate.

Intoxicated with his passion and the hopes it led to, Archie cast the tender note aside and forgot it quickly in the tumultuous whirl of daily growing certainty, till one day coming in from hunting he saw on the hall-table at Champ Royal a letter for him in Adéle's well-known writing. Starting as if he were stung he thrust it with an oath into his pocket, and glancing hastily round hurried to his room. Tearing it open with evil thoughts and looks, the only word that met his eye was one. 'Twas simply, " Come."

When such men lose their heads and strike they spare not sex nor any tie that binds the hand of others. Anger is a potent source of harm to him who is the victim of its presence, but the greater demon, in his hideous deeds, is fear. Archie knew that if his intrigue with Adéle were discovered he must bid farewell to Clarice. With brutal selfishness, born of panic, he determined therefore to sever himself at once, and all hazards, from what had come to be a moral and perpetual nightmare to him.

Conceive what Adéle suffered when she had read his last most callous words.

"For the second time you have broken my strict injunction to refrain from writing. I had good reason for it. You have chosen to ignore everything but the gratification of your own wishes, regardless of what may be the consequences to me. It is evident that I cannot rely upon you. Perhaps it is as well that I have made this discovery now. You will understand how useless it is to address me, as if you had a right to do so, when I tell you that Miss Beauchamp has consented to be my wife.

"My agents in Paris will henceforth pay you monthly double the allowance I have hitherto made to you. And if there be any other way in which I can meet your wishes with regard to your future comfort I shall be obliged if you will address them on the subject.

"L."

Stunned by the cruelly sudden and unexpected blow, Adéle was saved some hours of agony by the merciful insensibility into which she fell on first reading it. But with returning consciousness the poor dulled brain sadly and wearily woke to the fact that there was a sorrow, heavy beyond endurance, hanging over it, and was not content until with persistent, clamorous cries it had forced the short but too brutal tale back into her memory.

For a time it seemed as if the stupor into which she sank would end in the death it so closely counterfeited. But, with a strength hitherto unknown because uncalled for, she rallied, and as she gradually swept away the tangling thoughts, there came a change which made her look, as indeed she was, a different creature.

"So this is what you played, and I was but a pawn, to be cast away that you might win the queen. Good; but if I loved with all my strength I can hate with equal force. And by the gods of both the passions you shall learn which has the greatest power to slay."

And as she started to her feet, clenching her

small white hands, while her raven hair in falling masses brought out in fierce relief the pallid face and glittering eyes, Master Archie, dauntless as he doubtless was, might well have shrunk if he had known how nearly allied are the senses which dominate the lives of men.

"Ah, he has played boldly, but not wisely. Had he only waited he might have found me silent as the grave." Poor child. She shudders as the word slips from her. "But now. If it were my last act, there is yet time for sweet revenge." Once more the fierce, hot desert-blood sweeps through her veins; and, as she writes, her passion-working face bodes little happiness for Archie, if her bolt should hit the mark.

"Monsieur,

"A wretched victim of a love which for its own purposes did not scruple to use me as a tool to destroy your happiness while it worked for his, I write to tell you that, by the desire of your cousin, Colonel Campbell, the letters to and from you and Miss Beauchamp found their way to him through me. Should they not have reached their destination you will understand why.

"This may reach you yet in time to save his winning her by sowing sorrow and mistrust between you.

"I pray it may be so. For me it matters not. But—vengeance apart—I would undo the wrong I unwittingly took part in.

"My name is,

"ADÉLE."

The legend on this fiery arrow bore it safely to Calcutta, where it was found by Charlie on the eve of sailing home.

True woman, hardly was it gone beyond recovery, ere she would have given all she could command to call it back. She knew she had dealt a death-blow to all her hopes or chance of future love from Archie. And from that moment her earthly days were numbered.

There were times when, sinking pride and every other restraining feeling, she would gladly have cast herself at Archie's feet and asked his leave to let her die there if he would only look upon her kindly. But in an instant the letter she had sent to Charlie, every word of which was burnt into her brain, forbade the hope of peace or pardon, and she prayed for death as only those can do who know there is neither to be found on earth.

Smarting under the castigation which came yet more from Eila's looks than words, Archie had taken his *congé* with such grace as made her somewhat sorry for the fate which at once had torn from him love and fortune.

Sensitive as such men so often are—for, doubtful of themselves, in keen appreciation of their own shortcomings to which they cannot shut their eyes, they see in every glance or whisper a reflection of their feeling—Archie could not stay in London.

The buffeting at Eila's hands had shattered

all his easy confidence. Like that of many self-reliant men, it was strong enough until a firmer hand had grasped it. Friends, to whom he could turn with certainty of sympathy in the hour of trouble, he had none; for his selfish character had created a great desert in which there was not one oasis in which he might hope to find the shade and water which the hand of trusty fellowship is at such a time—to those who find the wave of falling fortune has cast them on the barren reef of disappointed hopes.

As the wounded stag might look in vain for aught but death from any of his rivals, yet hope to find a hind more kindly, so Archie's sick and wearied heart turned instinctively to Adéle.

She at least was always loving, and, as a certainty of the passionate reception she would give him came surging through his brain, he grasped the thought of going to her as does the famished traveller the prospect of the food and rest he so sorely needs.

In his state of exaggerated self-depreciation

the remembrance of her clinging devotion, and the picture he drew of the *abandon* with which she would welcome him, was the mental pabulum his wounded vanity and injured self-respect demanded. And with little loss of time he found himself in Paris.

Poor Adéle! The letter she had written in her fit of jealous anger had been most bitterly and incessantly regretted; and as she lay in the room, which she never quitted now, the memory of her brief history of happy love came swirling round continuously to the hour when she had cut away all hopes by her own mad hand. No thought or prospect of seeing him again was there to help to stay the rapid march of death, who with daily increasing strides came nigher to the victim so little loth to meet him. And at last her wasting life hung but by a hair which any breath of wind or jarring accident might sever.

Thus it was that Archie found her.

There are some crimes which bring with them

their own felt punishments, and there are those who maintain that the atonement here is so severe that the doctrine of eternal torture is but an exaggeration of it. For Archie it might well be said that his began when calling in the Rue du Bac his *nonchalant* air in asking for Mademoiselle was severely checked by the staid old servant, who, as he ushered him to the *salon*, told him, in a few curt but pregnant sentences, the sad state into which she had now fallen.

"*Mon Dieu! Monsieur le Colonel, elle vit! Mais on ne sait pas jusqu'à quand sa vie sera prolongée,*" were the words with which he was left to chew the cud of bitterest reflections.

"What? Adéle dying! Impossible! She so full of life and fire and passion! He had surely but to touch her hand and bid her live for him and her love would conquer all her weakness. Had he not proved to the uttermost its strength?" And his thoughts fly back to their first meetings in this very room, when in all the wealth of her young beauty she had shown that he was at least most welcome, to the tokens of growing interest she had evinced in his every word and look, to the intoxicating flashes of her love-beseeching eyes, as their intimacy grew, until at length she had fired his colder nature, and they drank together of the philter which so often ends in death—of love at least—to the one who has quaffed most deeply the bewitching poison.

Plunged deep in visions of the past which such memories call up, and realizing now all that he has thrown away, he begins to taste some of the bitterness which will pursue him with increasing strength until his expiation may be accepted.

"*Mademoiselle Adèle vous attend, Monsieur,*" says the attendant sorrowing servant, and brings him back to present woe and all he must go through.

As he enters the darkened room a *sœur* glides by him, and whispering words of caution leaves it. Ere his unaccustomed eye has pierced the gloom, the well-known voice—but oh! so changed —falters out the name she gave him in their early love—"Mon Louis!" Guided by the sound, he sees at last Adéle. Stretched on a couch, in purest white, without a trace of colour in her pinched and sadly worn face, it needs no learned opinion to lead him to the awful truth. She is indeed upon the brink of what we all must come to.

The next moment he is kneeling by her side, while she half-rising winds once more her arms around his neck, and is at peace such as she has never known before for a few brief seconds.

Alas! that they should be so short, the las on earth.

"Adéle! *Mon ange!* What is this I see?" at length he murmurs, forgetting, as men will, all that he has done, in the dread witness of its terrible results.

"*Mon cœur!* 'Tis nothing, since you are here at last. If you had but come a little sooner it might not have been. *Dieu sait!* But He is very good since He has sent you now, for one last kiss, to close my sad and weary eyes, which have looked—ah! how they have looked in vain for this. Louis! you never knew how I have longed for you, or you might have waited. But a little while and I would have been no more to trouble you or come across your truer, happier fate."

"Hush, child!" he whispers in a tone of pain which thrills through her with a joy that bids her struggle for dear life, as the long-forbidden hope flies back and knocks again for entrance to the swept and empty heart. "You know not what you say. I have no happier love than yours."

"What?" she cries in ecstasy of blissful wonderment, as the gladsome words dance through the doubting ear and fill her brain with mad, bewildering emotions. "Oh, Louis, what have I done?" she adds, as the memory of the letter she has sent to Charlie returns and bids her tremble for her new-found blessedness.

"'Tis not you, *ma bien aimée*, who should say that, 'tis I," answers the repentant Archie, as he fondly strokes the head she has buried in his breast.

"You know not what I have done, *chéri!* Alas, alas!" she cries with exceeding bitterness, as she recognizes all the consequences to him, to her, of that one fatal act, the only deed with which she can reproach herself; but oh! enough to countervail the wealth of love she so ungrudgingly has given. "He must know it now. He shall not feel I feared to tell him. But oh! it's death to love from him, I know," she thinks, as lying still she takes one last long draught of earthly bliss, and then she says in the firm accents of despair, with which is blended such true pathos as must make the listening angels weep—

"Louis!—you wrote and cast me off without one word of love. You maddened me with raging jealousy. I was not myself; oh! I was not myself, believe me, when I did it; for from that moment I have bitterly repented the irrevocable impulse, born of the only instant I have ever been in thought, in truth, in deed, not yours. But, alas! that I should have to say it, I flung a pebble into the pool of your fair fame, and I know not when or where the circling wave may reach. I wrote to your cousin and I told him—that—you had made me—take—his—letters—"

"What?" cries Archie, springing to his feet, and casting her from his arms in a paroxysm of sudden fear and fury. "You betrayed me? You false and—"

Happily for his hopes of future peace his eyes fall on her dress ere the cruel words are spoken, and the swelling torrent from her blood-stained lips seal his in time.

One lingering look, eloquent of pitying and forgiving love, meets his glance of horror, and then, the saddened eyelids closing, the most wretched and remorseful man is left alone indeed.

CHAPTER XII.

"A brave vessel, who had no doubt some noble creatures in her dash'd all to pieces,"—*Miranda*.

GALLE was left behind, and as the sun went down the passengers on board the 'Kandy' were grouped together on the poop to enjoy a little exercise on deck, without the feeling of being in a vapour-bath forthwith.

Among those who rather fraternized with Amy and her fellow-travellers were Sir Octavius and Lady Coppinger. He, a Bengal civilian, lately the ruler of a country thrice the size of Ireland, was going home, after an absence during which at least one generation had matured, to sink into the existence which is so inevitably and terribly petty for the declining years of our great proconsuls. Notwithstanding his long, hard-worked career, no one would have imagined from his tall straight figure, the ruddy, clean-shaved face, the bright and vigorous eye, that he had lived so long in that much-abused climate. The secret lay in continuous mental and physical activity.

Lady Coppinger, though she might have been well younger, was still a very handsome specimen of the Anglo-Indian lady, who, having originally great beauty, has not been allowed by her numerous admirers to forget anything which might add to the successful resistance of the great enemy of female charms. Married for a short time before to a dashing cavalry soldier, she had experienced enough of the inconvenience of insufficient means not to allow the offer of the rising civilian to be inconsiderately refused.

Bidding farewell to a numerous suite of sighing adorers, she, coming on board at Calcutta, had cast her eyes impatiently over the halt, maimed, and generally decrepit-looking males who formed the principal portion of the steamers' living freight. As she did so her glance fell upon a group, which, standing aloof, at once attracted her attention by the extraordinary beauty of the lady, the air of distinction of the men.

"Octavius, my dear, I am so sorry to trouble you; but now that I have not Hervey, or Cyrus, or Taddy, or anyone near me, I must, for the present at least. Do find out for me who those people are."

"Which, my beloved?"

"Why, those, of course," she answers impatiently, pointing towards Amy and her friends, who were gazing with mingled feelings at what they all felt was their last view of a place which had seen their first steps in a country so fatal to more than one dear to them.

Returning with the desired information, and an air as if protesting against such unaccustomed servitude, he is rewarded by her saying:

"Thanks, dearest. I am so sorry to have given you the trouble. Doubtless I shall soon find somebody to be useful. How stupid of

Hervey not to come home with us. Those men are always thinking of themselves. Elliot, did you say? I wonder now if that can be a son of an old friend of mine. Get them introduced to you, Octavius. If they are as nice as they look we shall find them pleasant companions." So saying, she sweeps down below and is no more seen for a day or two.

Then, sufficiently recovered from a renewed acquaintance with the troubles of sea-life, so hateful to many, Lady Coppinger sails on deck, armed and ready for such conquest as may be open to her. Attended by her obedient husband, who begins to find his new position of *cavaliere servente* to his *exigeante* dame rather trying to his temper and views of his own independence, she speedily discovers the same *quartette* grouped on the shady side of the deck.

"Well, my dear, have you found out who they are? Soldiers evidently."

"Yes, darling. I have made their acquaintance. She is charming."

"Doubtless! I want to know the men. Introduce them to me."

"I am afraid, love, that, as it is, I must ask you to come with me then, for I can hardly break in upon them and bring the young fellows here."

With an impatient shrug of her shoulders the ex-queen submits to the indignity, and the introduction all round is duly effected.

Since then the intimacy has ripened with the rapidity of constant companionship on board ship, and Sir Octavius finds to his intense relief that his new duties are transferred to another, and that he is at liberty to devote himself to Amy, with greater satisfaction to himself, be it said in truth, when Charlie smokes the weed for which poor Paul finds it so hard to obtain leave from his imperious and demonstrative friend.

A few well-put, though well-bred, questions had speedily made her mistress of all the information she desired, and confirmed the impression she had formed at first, which in due time she might act upon. Meanwhile, *vogue la galère!* And every one at all disposed to be sociable was on the best of terms with the ship, its officers, the surroundings, and the others.

There are several stages in the lives of those on board a passenger-steamer — indifference, acquaintance, friendship, love, or deadly hatred.

Happily, or otherwise, the last seldom endures beyond the termination of the voyage. Lady Coppinger had arrived somewhat quickly at the second one, and, judging by appearances, is well on her way in the tender phase of the fourth.

"Good evening, Captain," she says, addressing the autocrat of the moment as he emerges from his cabin on deck. "I hope we are going to have fine weather now until we get to Suez?"

"If I could ensure it, you certainly might command it, my Lady," says the skipper, with a sweep of his cap, for he fancies himself rather. "But there is a fall in the glass which I don't quite like. For all that it looks so fair just now, we may find ourselves in very different circumstances to-morrow."

"That's not a pleasant forecast, Captain Firebrace," says Ronald. "However, there is plenty of sea-room, as you call it, I imagine?"

"At present ample, and to-night we should pass about a hundred miles to the south'ard of the Laccadives."

"I hope you won't make a mistake and run us on one of them!"

"No fear, Sir Octavius. Though if we did, as they are all coral-reefs, and there is only about an eighth of an inch of iron between us and the bottom, I think it would fare badly with us—so I am not likely to commit such a blunder," quoth the skipper, somewhat huffily, walking aft to the binnacle.

"That is pleasant to hear, Captain Elliot! Fancy a bit of sharp rock running like a knife along the ship's side, and laying us open to the sea like a gigantic oyster! Ugh!"

"It would be startling! But old Firebrace

seems to know his work. Let us hope he will do it."

The day is just breaking next morning when all on board the 'Kandy' are startled by a sudden shock, and then a hard grating sound, which makes her tremble from stem to stern—followed by quick shouts of "Stop her!" "Back her!" "Hard astern!"—and for a few terrible moments, full of anxiety even to the boldest, who recognize what it means, all is motionless silence. Then arise cries from a few of the ladies, women, and some of the weaker men, bedridden for the time, as the steamer, happily firmly fixed on the ledge to which she has been carried by her momentum, bumps uneasily on her side, while the heavy seas break over her.

With the calmness of ignorance of danger, many passengers remained below dressing and securing their valuables, while others, in all the terror and *déshabille* of rudely-disturbed slumbers, rushed on deck, much to the discomfiture of the more sober-minded. One obese dame, swathed in her husband's flannel jacket and knickerbockers, refused to leave the deck to change her costume, while more than one fair creature seemed insensible either to the rude wind or ruder gaze to which their unprotected limbs were so much exposed.

As might have been expected, Amy behaved with perfect *sang froid*. Dressing quickly and suitably as soon as she had realized the situation, she put several things together in a bag with her watch and other trinkets, and waited patiently for Charlie's guidance.

Gaining the deck on the first alarm, he had quickly seen the danger of remaining below, for apparently at any moment a roller larger than his fellows might suck the steamer back into the depths from which the coral springs. She meets him at the door of the cabin as he calls her name.

"I am quite ready, and not at all frightened since you are here," she says, in answer to his anxious questioning, with a sweet, sad smile which haunts him in years to come. When they get up the hatchway they find Ronald attending to the requirements of Lady Coppinger, with as much *empressement* as if being cast away on a desert-looking island were of daily occurrence.

"I have everything now, I think," she is saying to her husband, "but 'Gyp.' She, you know, was consigned to the care of the butcher by that horrid purser's order. So would you mind, dear, going and getting her for me?"

Sir Octavius looks doubtfully at the acrobatic kind of path before him; but essentially a man of pluck and action, in another minute he is clambering along the side of the heaving, wrecking ship, and with a kindly boldness which is not copied by younger owners of their dogs, he rescues the terrier from a watery death, and presently comes back triumphant with the little grateful Skye clinging to his arms. Even Lady Coppinger is moved.

Meanwhile the captain, bareheaded, coatless, shoeless, as he had sprung out from his cabin on the first astounding shout, was giving rapid orders, which were being carried out as well as might be expected from a crew of Lascars with only a sprinkling of English mates and quartermasters. A hawser is attached by an Indian swimmer to a palm-tree on the island, about a cable's length away, and by clinging to it from the bows and stern of a large life-boat it is hoped that the passengers may be conveyed in safety to the shore ere the ship breaks up.

"Ladies first," cries the skipper. "You must look sharp! No, Sir Octavius, 'tis impossible. They must trust themselves to my officers. If you want to take care of Lady Coppinger every one would have a plausible reason for trying to go first also. I quite appreciate your motive, but it must be so."

"Very well, Captain Firebrace; but it seems to me a terrible risk. If anything happens to that boat in such a surf with only two men in it there will be a heavy responsibility attached to you."

"I accept it. Shove off, Mr. Clarkson!"

The next moment the precious freight, including Amy, is being warped under the lee of the wreck towards the land. And for some anxious minutes all goes well till they are about midway, when a tremendous roller sweeping round the stern catches the life-boat suddenly with such vehemence that the hawser is torn from the hands of the man in the bows, she broaches to, and the next instant all are struggling in the surf. Charlie and Paul ere this have seen the too evident danger, and kicking off their shoes stand ready with life-buoys in their hands for the catastrophe they too surely dread. With one accord they plunge into the seething water and make for the helpless ladies, who fortunately are swept inshore. Several men follow their example, and as the two sailors had been selected for their powers of swimming, only six of the unhappy occupants of the boat are missing, when breathless and drenched the survivors try to thank their gallant rescuers.

"Charlie! to owe my life to you is indeed to make it doubly sweet. What instinct brought you to me? Surely I was sinking?"

"I kept my eye on the red feather in your hat, and it was no great distance to get to you. What I feared most was a shark; they don't often meet with such a dainty morsel," he says quickly, to try and check the rising tide of hysterical emotion. "But what is this?" as a tumultuous rush of naked natives comes down upon them.

Happily they are peacefully inclined, and, swimming like the fish they live on, the life-boat soon is righted, and working back along the cable, gains the helpless hulk, from which without further misadventure the rest of the passengers are landed.

Quickly ascertaining where they are, the captain calls for volunteers, and before the sun has set a boat is making its way for the mainland, about four hundred miles distant.

"I hope those fine fellows may reach it, Paul;

otherwise we may eat our Christmas dinner here. The skipper says the cyclone drove us at least a hundred miles out of our course; so we are not likely to be picked up by any passing ship."

"There was not much of a cyclone near us, Charlie. Bad seamanship brought us here. But taking the most lively view of the chances of that small open boat getting safely across, it will be some time before a steamer gets down here from Bombay."

By dint of much hard work and great good fortune in the ship holding together, weakly iron-built as she was, sufficient food was saved to give one meal a day; as she began to break up the baggage was washed ashore, and much incongruous raiment adorned the castaways.

It was a curious phase of life. Successful publicans from Shanghai and diggers from Australia mingled for a time with the "aristocrats," as they called those hailing from Calcutta and Madras. But at last, familiarity breeding its proverbial consequences, Charlie making friends with the petty Rajah who ruled the island, got a small shanty knocked up for Lady Coppinger and Amy. With the aid of a ship's punkah he, Ronald, and the Weasel kept them pretty free from heat and yet more fiery language.

"Ah, Charlie, I wish sometimes that we might be left here always. I quite dread going back into the world."

"Don't say that! You know how glad my mother will be to see you, and when we are once more at Amat you will get rid of these morbid fancies which cling to you too much."

Amy shakes her head most sadly, and her eyes are filled with blinding tears as she says, "When one is happiest one fears the most. It is only the miserable who can enjoy the luxury of hope."

"You are paradoxical this morning! You are getting into a nervous state from want of food and proper rest. I trust the boat has got to the mainland, and then our relief cannot be far off. Come, and call upon the Rajah. I have promised him one of my red jackets in return for his building you this small palace."

With much ceremony, Charlie buttons his sea-stained doublet round a part of the corpulent Chief, who in return presents Amy with his state umbrella, adorned with a lock of his coarse black hair—which she accepts with a pretty smile, saying to Charlie, " It is not quite your taste? It certainly is not mine, and yet this crimson shade may be made the fashion. Shall we try?"

So laughingly they wander back along the beach and throw pebbles in. Their hearts fly back to younger days, and their spirits, rising, drift into the happy cloudland whence comes the unearthly mirth filling those about to die. *Credat* the Western Highlander.

The consciousness of this smites Charlie with a fearful chill, as after one of her most lively sallies she suddenly stops, grows deadly pale, and pointing to the north, says in a low and awe-struck tone: " Oh, Charlie! It is coming! I see it! Help me against it if you can. Alas!

I know you cannot." And in a trance-like state she falls into his arms.

How long she remained so he never knew; but, as it seemed, an age after he suddenly saw a small black cloud of smoke. Presently there was no doubt. It was a steamer, and from her course must be the relief so long expected.

She was a terribly small craft to crowd into the numerous passengers of the stately 'Kandy'; but there was no help for it, the only way of getting accommodation for the ladies was by much packing, and Lady Coppinger kindly shared with Amy the wretched cabin apportioned as a state apartment to the Indian magnate's wife. As they neared the rock of Aden the heat increased and at times became almost unbearable.

"I fear, my dear, that you will find it still worse in the Red Sea. It is quite awful there at this time of year, and in this cockle-shell I don't know how you will bear it. You are looking terribly pulled down."

Amy's only answer is a sickly smile.

It was very true. The 'Beaver,' originally built for the North American trade, was quite unfitted for the purpose to which she was now applied, and after passing the Straits of Bab-el-Mandeb she became a sort of furnace which scorched the vital organs of many of the already feeble passengers.

Poor Amy, never very strong, had suffered more from her immersion and the hardships on the island than she allowed the others to know, and at last found herself in a state of high fever.

Struggling on deck one evening in the hope of a little 'cool air,' she frightened Charlie by her haggard looks, the incoherence of her manner.

"Charlie, dear!" she says at last, bursting into tears, "I cannot help it—I feel as if I were going to leave you to-night. My brain seems on fire, and all power to live is burnt out of me."

"Keep up only for two days more and we shall be at Suez, they say. And then we shall soon find ourselves in reach of all you need, poor darling."

"Ah, Charlie, I fear it is too late. From the first moment I saw this ship coming for us a dread instinct warned me of the end which I feel is very near now."

"Don't give way so, dear heart! You are only full of fever and the fancies it creates. I will go and ask the Captain if he will do what I believe has sometimes answered. If we steam back for a little time we may get some air by meeting the slight breeze which is following us. And, though it is prolonging the voyage, it may so cool the ship as to make it endurable."

For a few hours this was done, and Amy went below calmer, but leaving Charlie more than anxious. He had much need to be; for after the slight difference in temperature, produced by the manœuvre adopted by the considerate Captain, the heat became more insupportable than ever, and several of the passengers died through the night in consequence.

The day was dawning when shriek after shriek rang through the ship. Hurrying aft, the doctor and stewardess traced the cries to Lady Coppinger's cabin, in which she stood alone as they entered, followed by Charlie in all the agonies of direst apprehension.

"What is the matter, my Lady?"

"Can you ask? Look there!"

At first nothing was to be seen in the empty berth, by the widely open port-hole to which she pointed with terrifying significance; but the doctor, approaching it more closely, froze the blood of the horror-stricken Charlie as he sprang up, and, seizing a shred of linen which hung on the projecting latch of the outlying deadlight, cried out:

"My God! She has fallen overboard!"

One great sorrow drives out its predecessor, happily for mortals, or the accumulation would be beyond our strength.

How Charlie lived through the time immediately following the awful accident which so verified poor Amy's forebodings he could never tell.

Mercifully for us all, great and unexpected blows, physical or mental, bring with them an anodynous stupor which deadens first the shock, and then gives nature time to recover the elasticity which permits us on the morrow to look upon the poignant grief of to-day with a strength of resignation, sometimes mistaken for heartlessness.

Thus Charlie arriving at Alexandria found a telegram, delivered by the Consul's kindly aid, which, arresting his new-born sorrow, sent his thoughts flying homewards with intense anxiety. It was from his father, and with the terrible curtness of such messages left too much to the imagination. Perhaps it was as well. It said:

"Clarice, overwhelmed by the news of your marriage and despairing of your safety, was struck down by brain fever. Her life still hangs upon a thread. Be prepared for the worst. Your arrival telegraphed from Suez."

Poor Charlie! It seemed as if he were to pay in a few short days the condensed debt of compensating sorrow for all the joyousness of the life in which it had been so long absent.

Ronald, who was with him at the moment, seeing by his stricken aspect that something more than commonly grievous had been communicated to him in the telegram, with the familiarity of an old friend takes it from his nerveless hand.

"Poor fellow!" is his mental ejaculation. "This is an awful combination. What can have given rise to it?" Then pulling himself together he tries to do the same by Charlie.

"Look here, old man. There must be some mistake. If Miss Beauchamp was *accablée* by the news of your marriage and danger, she will certainly be sustained in her recovery by hearing of your present safety from both perils. Let me telegraph to the old gentleman, and by the time we get to Malta I lay you a monkey to nothing that you hear she is no longer depressed in mind or body."

"As you will, Paul. I hope it may be so; but I feel as if it were too late."

"Not a bit. Bear up, and you will find I am right."

In a few minutes Ronald has written and despatched the following message to Lord Amat, as from Charlie.

"Not married; was bringing home Mrs. Gardenne, who was lost. Terribly anxious about Clarice. Let me hear at Malta. Will go home by Marseilles."

Returning, he meets the purser of the 'Marsala,' who says, "I think there must be some mistake in the list of passengers. I do not like to trouble Captain Grant, who seems terribly cut up. Can you tell me the name of the poor lady who fell out of the port on board the 'Beaver'? I understand she was called Mrs. Gardenne. Here," pointing to his official list, "there is no such person; but 'Captain and Mrs. Grant' are bracketted together."

"By Jove! that explains the mystery. I can't say, Mr. Simons, how the mistake has happened, except that my friend's servant took the passages in Calcutta for poor Mrs. Gardenne and her maid as well; and the intelligent Baboo clerk may have jumped over quickly to conclusions. But let me have the list for a little. The mistake has already given rise to much annoyance if not worse, and I want to show how it has probably reached his people in England."

As Ronald expected, the tonic of the fresh anxiety helped Charlie to brace himself to bear the irremediable sorrow, and by the time they neared Malta he was counting the hours ere he could hear from home.

Hurrying up to the Post Office he found a bundle of letters and telegrams waiting for him; but the most precious of all was a brief message from Clarice. "Much better. Alas! alas! poor Amy! Writing to you at Hôtel du Louvre, Paris. All well, and looking forward beyond words to seeing you again."

How Paul and he blessed the inventor who has annihilated time and space. But for the telegraph what further complications might not have happened? Among other things it decided Sir Octavius also to go home through France; and Lady Coppinger, who since poor Amy's death had changed very much, and at first secluded herself entirely, one evening, as their momentous voyage drew to a close, sent for Ronald to go and see her.

With a very different manner from that which had been habitual to her, she told him to sit down, and thus addressed him: "Captain Elliot, when you told me who you were you confirmed an intense desire, only waiting for the long deferred opportunity of going home, to try and see justice done to your poor mother."

Ronald started.

"Ah! I forgot. Of course you don't know who I am. Did you ever hear of Gertrude Leigh, who married Maurice Fitzgerald?"

"Only too often, Lady Coppinger," replies Ronald with concentrated bitterness.

"My task is harder than I fancied," she thinks, "but I must go through with it now."

"Well," she continued aloud, "I am afraid from your tone that it was not so pleasantly as she might have wished! Or, I had better be frank at once and say, I—for she became Mrs. Coppinger, and is now—myself!"

For a few seconds Ronald is struck dumb. "This the woman whose thoughtless levity, if no worse, had caused such pain to his dear mother; such years of fathomless jealous grief to his father; such shame and sorrow to himself?" It needed all his power of self-control to maintain the silence which he felt could alone enable him to spare her the bitter punishment she deserved.

At last she breaks it herself. "I can well understand all you think of me; but, believe me, I have for years grieved over the consequences of my weakness in listening to the specious pretexts of the scoundrel who used his power over poor frightened women by trying to extort money from them. I will not weary you with details; but again I say, believe that I sorrowed for my friend Ada's memory more than I can tell you, when it reached me that your father drew such inferences from the solitary instance of her absence from home."

"But why did you not write to him, Lady Coppinger?"

"It was not for two years after your poor mother's death, when I saw his second marriage announced, that I heard how he had treated you, and the reason alleged for it. I wrote to him at once and told him what you shall hear now, and what it is my purpose to tell him when we reach England."

"Did he never answer you?"

"No; my letter was returned with the words: 'Opened for the address. The excuses of such a person cannot be believed, and therefore are unread.' Of course after that I felt that it was useless to write again, and that I must wait until we met face to face. I married again, shortly after, and have never left India or my husband, who preferred to stay out there until he could come home for good."

"My unhappy father! He seemed bent on depriving himself of all possibility of comfort."

"It is the way of such men. Unreasoning jealousy feeds upon itself, and refuses evidence which would prove the lie of its existence! However, let me now tell you what really took place."

"I think, Lady Coppinger," says Ronald, touched by her evident sorrow for his mother whose memory has always been so sacred to him, and her determination to make her own penitence practical, "you may spare yourself much detail to me, though it may be well for you to give the fullest particulars to my father. We are at last, I am happy to say, on the terms we ought to be. The news of my wounds in India seemed to soften his heart, for he sent for my dear mother's old maid, Hotham, listened to her plain, straightforward tale, and wrote to me a letter which showed that after all it was more his head than his heart which was accountable for the misery of the past."

"I am so glad to hear it. It makes it comparatively easy for me to tell what I know. Briefly, I was young, inexperienced, and easily imposed upon. Poor Ada's cousin told me a plausible tale, and I was made an unconscious instrument of his attempt to get her into his power, and thus make her a convenient means of supplying him with money. I did not know this until some time afterwards, when another victim of his, who had been weak enough to be fascinated by his undoubted charms of mind and body—and to give him written proofs thereof!—had the courage to turn round at last and defy him.

"Your mother, with more *savoir faire*, perhaps, saw through his design. I know not. But at all events, in answer to a farewell letter which I had written to her in ignorance of the man's villainous plot, she came with Hotham to Southampton to my intense surprise; and, sending for me to her hotel just as we were about to sail, reproached me in the most bitter language. I confess I was so stung by what she said that I answered her hotly, and we parted on anything but friendly terms. It was not long after that I heard of her death. Then followed the interval spoken of, and my attempt to let Sir Claude know the facts."

"I fear," says Ronald, taking her hand, "that I too have often done you an injustice. I am sure, from what you say and from what I have seen of you in the last few weeks, that it is impossible you could wilfully have done what my poor mother and father thought. But he never does things by halves, I know, and when we get home he will accept what you have to say in a manner which will wipe away as much as is possible all that is unpleasant. What a scoundrel that fellow Davenport must have been! Do you know what became of him?"

"He died miserably in Calcutta, having at last caught a Tartar in the husband of the poor woman, who, goaded to desperation by his leech-like conduct, defied him and threw herself, not in vain, on the merciful consideration of the one she should have trusted sooner. He was horsewhipped at the Band one evening, kicked out of his regiment forthwith, and died not long afterwards a pauper and an outcast."

"Thank God!" ejaculates Ronald, with much fervour.

CHAPTER XIII.

"Sigh no more, ladies, sigh no more, men were deceivers ever."
Balthazar.

FASCINATED by the dancing letters, Clarice had read on, in another account of the loss of the 'Kandy,' until she saw the list of passengers, and that 'the survivors,' as it was cruelly briefly put, would not arrive in England for a month. Then, feeling as if the world were sinking from her, she fell from her chair.

The General, alone with her at breakfast, was at first too startled to take in what had happened. Summoning her maid, the ordinary restoratives were applied in vain, until at last the Doctor was sent for. His quick professional eye soon discovered how serious was the attack, and with her father's help she was carried up to bed.

"There must have been some great mental shock, sir. What was it?"

"Heaven knows! We were by ourselves, and had hardly exchanged our usual greetings when she took up the paper, and presently, when I looked round on hearing a noise, she was lying on the floor!"

"Strange! Let me see what she was studying. Ah!" exclaims the Doctor, as he glances rapidly over the journal. "Forgive the question, but, have you any one in India in whom you, or rather perhaps she, may be much interested?"

"Yes! She was engaged to Captain Grant in the Red Highlanders."

"You don't say that! No wonder, then, poor thing!"

"Why? What is the matter, Doctor?"

"That!" answers the man of medicine, curtly and emphatically, as he puts his finger on the telegraphic announcement of the wreck, followed by the names of those on board.

"This is a climax with a vengeance!" ejaculates the General, who, like many fathers under similar circumstances, has not dived very deeply into the mysteries of his daughter's *affaires*. "Married another!—and lost in every sense! Poor Clarice! Poor Charlie! What can have brought it about?" he mutters to himself as he thinks over much which has seemed so strange to him for long.

At last the Doctor discreetly rouses him, saying: "Does Mrs. Beauchamp know this, General?"

"I think not."

"Well, I should go and break it gently to her, for she will probably feel it much; and I shall want her help, I fear, ere we can see your daughter well again."

"You don't mean that her illness is more serious than a fainting fit?"

"I do indeed, I grieve to say I did not

like her looks from the first, but now I am afraid we shall have to nurse her through a dangerous fever!"

It was too true! Weakened and depressed by long and increasing anxiety, she had no strength to stand against this crushing stroke, and it needed all the skill and care they could secure to hold the golden bowl together. But the struggle was severe and very doubtful until the well-considered telegram, flashing home from Ronald, brought, as he had prophesied, the only ally that could incline the scale to victory.

* * * * *

"Eila, darling! Does it strike you that I am looking very ill? Will he think me thin, yellow, hideous?" is the anxious question one morning as they sit in the convalescent's charming boudoir.

"I can hardly say what his taste may have arrived at after two years spent in such a climate, where, they say, everyone becomes so dark and orange-hued! Remembering that you had the advantage of being 'personally engaged,' as the domestic puts it, while I have been secured by letter only, I confess I should not mind exchanging my painfully robust appearance for that air of delicacy which makes you so interesting just now."

"Nonsense!" replies Clarice, blushing most becomingly. "You know Captain Elliot says he only refrained at Amat from adding to your list of victims because of Sir Claude's eccentric conduct. So you have no need to be anxious."

"Perhaps I might say I have had my share of that already!"

"Ah! Can I forget? It has been a terrible two years for all of us. And now, when it seems as if happiness were almost within our grasp, I tremble sometimes lest the unforeseen should dash it from us."

"Let me see!" says Eila, rather dreading any trial of her shattered nerves, and producing a letter posted at Marseilles. "Ronald writes: 'We shall remain only one day in Paris, just to get a few things for our kit, to prevent being turned away as tramps from the door! So that in twenty-four hours after you get this I hope in person to—' Oh, the rest is nonsense!" she adds, as she hurriedly folds up the paper with an access of colour which tells much.

"To-morrow?" says Clarice, with a dreamy look in her sweet, soft eyes. "And now it has come to that! Oh! I think if I could have foreseen all that I have gone through since Charlie left me at Amat, I could not have let him go without me."

"It is very well for us that we cannot see too far or too much," answers Eila, cheerily. "What have I not been saved, for example, by my ignorance of Ronald's family skeleton, so happily buried! He tells me that Lady Coppinger is overcome with remorse, and burning to see Sir Claude, who is good enough to say he does not require any further proof that he was too long a fool!"

"How small the world is! What a strange

chance that poor Lady Elliot's old friend should have come home with Ronald!"

"Yes; and that, from what he lets drop, she should have carried on with him rather, at first! He says she is still very striking-looking and most agreeable."

"Doubtless! Probably she has had plenty of practice! What does poor Ralph say to all this?"

"I believe he is more taken up with his new bearskin than what you call 'all this!' But he professed to be quite consoled when I told him that if polyandry were permitted here, as Ronald says it is in the Himalayas, I would undoubtedly bear him in mind."

"Eila!"

"Oh, my dear! it's quite safe, I can assure you. The poor boy cannot go through another season without a *grande passion*, which will quite obliterate me from his thoughts."

"If he chooses an object as nice and wise as yourself, I can wish him nothing better, at his age. Have you seen or heard anything of the Campbells since I was laid up?"

"Ah, a good deal! Gilbert tells me that Archie dashed abroad the day after I saw him; that he has 'sent in his papers,' as they call it; that he, of all men in the world, has gone over to the Church of Rome, and talks of La Trappe!"

"Heavens! I wonder why?"

"I should not inquire too closely, Clarice. Lady Alice is furious with Fate. All her matrimonial plans being scattered, she has betaken herself with the girls to the Black Forest. They will have a dreary time of it, I fear."

"Poor things! Julia feels it more than Olive, I fancy."

"'Tis her nature. By-the-bye, Ronald asks me to look out for a rich wife for Mr. Fletcher, so that he can settle down somewhere near us. He says, 'he is' rather good-looking, an excellent fellow, and most amusing, as you will find when you know the Weasel.' Among his other attractions he is going to help to 'tie us up,' whatever that may mean!"

"He seems to be as fascinating as we have found some others of the regiment. I wonder if they are all so?"

"They should be labelled 'dangerous' if they are."

"They will lose one at least of their number. I must have Charlie all to myself when I get him!"

At this moment a demure-looking abigail enters, and with a suppressed smile delivers a card to Eila.

With a presence of mind which, under the circumstances, does her infinite credit, she rises calmly from her seat by the side of Clarice, saying, "Really, these people are very pertinacious! May I leave you for a minute, dear, to see this person down-stairs? I will be back presently;" and she quietly leaves the room.

Passing through the vestibule on her way to the library, Eila suddenly finds herself locked in the arms of a tall, bearded man, who makes no apology for embracing her so rapturously that some minutes elapse before she can extricate herself.

At last, without being altogether free, she manages to say, "Really, if this is the consequence of your being exposed to a burning sun for two years I may congratulate myself that you have stayed no longer in India."

"I could not help it, my darling, when I saw you. I didn't mean to, really. Forgive me, or I shall have to return what I confess I have taken without leave."

"Not at present, sir. But what have you done with your friend?"

"I left him in the library, and wandered out here in the hope of meeting you alone. The butler put me up to the ropes; and I thought you might reward me for my former self-control?"

"You have not improved by keeping! But stay here if you like, and I will see what can be done for you both. How is it, by-the-bye, that you are here to-day? You wrote that you were obliged to stay in Paris."

"Did I? I had clean forgotten that. Anyhow, the fact is we thought, as we were *en route*, it was a waste of time staying in such a desert as we found it; so here we are."

"I see. Poor Clarice! I hope she is strong enough to bear these sudden manœuvres. I daresay she will, though her lines have not been cast in the pleasantest places of late."

"You won't be long?" implores Ronald, in a tone which makes her smile as she moves away.

"Not very. But even for you"—and she gives him a look which rewards him for much of the past—"I cannot forget those two misguided ones who have so nearly paid an awful penalty for too ready a credulity, which has all but wrecked their happiness."

The next minute she is warmly welcoming Charlie.

"And Clarice is quite better now? She

won't be upset if I go and see her at once?" he asks, with a nervous manner which Eila contrasts favourably with the more assured air he carried when at Amat.

"Not if you are gentle, and avoid being too— abrupt!" she replies, blushing at her own late experience.

"Then may I— ?"

"Yes. Come with me."

Arrived at the door of Clarice's room, she knocks softly, opens it, looks in, and, beckoning to him, hears, as she closes it, the astonished, joyful cry of—

"Charlie?"

responded to in smothered, tenderest accents by—

"Clarice! my only love, at last———"

The martial drum is changed to peaceful bell,
And all is done, for now it endeth well.

"If it be true, that 'good wine needs no bush,'
'Tis true that a good play needs no Epilogue."—*Rosalind.*

EPILOGUE.

THE Autumn is yet at its best.

The West Highlands are steeped in the mellowed beauty which it brings.

The 'Cygnet' floats in graceful lines upon the light blue waters with an air of sprightly gaiety, as if rejoicing that she has on her wings borne back to their homeful nest her friends.

The morning sun is shining on the silvery woods, the purple hills, the glistening sea, and all Nature is bedecked in gladsome attire, when Charlie's mother, looking from her window to the terrace, sees him with his bride.

Turning to descend and join them she exclaims, "O God, I thank Thee! He has indeed come back to her, and Amat."

'Tis ten to one, this play can never please
All. . . .
All the expected good we are like to hear,
For this play at this time, is only in
The merciful construction of good women;
For such a one we show'd them : If they smile
And say 'twill do, I know, within a while
All the best men are ours; for 'tis ill hap,
If they hold, when their ladies bid them clap.
Epilogue, King Henry VIII.

THE END.

BUNGAY, SUFFOLK : CLAY AND TAYLOR, PRINTERS.

www.ingramcontent.com/pod-product-compliance
Lightning Source LLC
Chambersburg PA
CBHW021357230426
43666CB00006B/559